T0247695

Praise for *Never Play It Safe*

"Whoever tells you that the 'safe' path is the better path doesn't understand how life works. Fortunately, Chase Jarvis gets it right, and Never Play It Safe *serves as a radically simple blueprint to reclaim our creativity and personal power."*
—ROBERT GREENE, AUTHOR OF *The 48 Laws of Power*

"This book is a powerful compass for embracing risk and creativity in all aspects of life. Chase shows us how to step out of our comfort zones and become who we were meant to be."
—SOPHIA AMARUSO, SERIAL ENTREPRENEUR AND *New York Times* BESTSELLING AUTHOR OF *Girlboss*

"Trust yourself. No one else can do that for you. Chase Jarvis is a maker of magic and a weaver of possibility, and this book can unlock the future for you, if you'll let it."
—SETH GODIN, AUTHOR OF *The Song of Significance*

"*Everything that we all want in life—success, fulfillment, freedom, happiness—is on the other side of fear. And nobody helps us overcome this faster than my man Chase Jarvis does in this book.*"
—DAYMOND JOHN, CEO OF SHARK GROUP, CEO AND FOUNDER OF FUBU, AND A SHARK ON ABC'S *Shark Tank*

"*Chase Jarvis is one of the true helpers out there, speaking openly and honestly about what it takes to live the creative life. I've stolen so much inspiration from him over the years and so will you.*"
—AUSTIN KLEON, ARTIST AND AUTHOR OF *Steal Like an Artist*

"*Building a life you love doesn't happen on accident—it's a process. Few people know this like Chase Jarvis does, and* Never Play It Safe *is the roadmap.*"
—GARY VAYNERCHUK, SERIAL ENTREPRENEUR, CHAIRMAN OF VAYNERX, CEO OF VAYNERMEDIA, CEO OF VEEFRIENDS, AND FIVE-TIME *New York Times* BESTSELLING AUTHOR

Never Play It Safe

Also by Chase Jarvis

The Best Camera Is the One That's With You:
iPhone Photography

Seattle 100: Portrait of a City

Creative Calling: Establish a Daily Practice, Infuse Your
World with Meaning, and Succeed in Work + Life

Never Play It Safe

A Practical Guide to Freedom, Creativity, and a Life You Love

Chase Jarvis

HARPER
BUSINESS

An Imprint of HarperCollins*Publishers*

NEVER PLAY IT SAFE. Copyright © 2024 by Chase Jarvis, Inc. All rights reserved. Printed in the United States of America. No part of this book may be used or reproduced in any manner whatsoever without written permission except in the case of brief quotations embodied in critical articles and reviews. For information, address HarperCollins Publishers, 195 Broadway, New York, NY 10007.

HarperCollins books may be purchased for educational, business, or sales promotional use. For information, please email the Special Markets Department at SPsales@harpercollins.com.

FIRST EDITION

Designed by Michele Cameron

Library of Congress Cataloging-in-Publication Data
Names: Jarvis, Chase, author.
Title: Never play it safe : a practical guide to freedom, creativity, and a life you love / Chase Jarvis.
Description: First edition. | New York, NY : HarperBusiness, [2024]
Identifiers: LCCN 2024016170 (print) | LCCN 2024016171 (ebook) |
ISBN 9780062879998 (hardcover) | ISBN 9780062880024 (ebook)
Subjects: LCSH: Success. | Risk-taking (Psychology)
Classification: LCC BF637.S8 J347 2024 (print) | LCC BF637.
S8 (ebook) | DDC 158.1—dc23/eng/20240502
LC record available at https://lccn.loc.gov/2024016170
LC ebook record available at https://lccn.loc.gov/2024016171

24 25 26 27 28 LBC 5 4 3 2 1

For Kate

For your love and all your help
in finding my way back to myself.
Over and over again.

Contents

Read This First!

Security is mostly a superstition. It does not exist in nature, nor do the children of men as a whole experience it. Avoiding danger is no safer in the long run than outright exposure. Life is either a daring adventure, or nothing.

—HELEN KELLER

Safety is an illusion.

It does not exist in nature, so why then do we seek it? Why do we believe it is essential for a good life when in reality the pursuit of safety is what keeps us from feeling the most alive?

Look into your soul for a moment. Think of the mind you've got, the head on your shoulders, and the body you were born with. The heart that beats in your chest underneath all the products and the layers of everything that the world piles on you . . . and that you pile on yourself. Think about it.

Deep down, do you really believe that you were meant to play it safe? To stay in a little box defined by someone else?

Hell no. Deep down, you know it's all risky, so why not just go for it?

You were built to be dynamic. You were built for challenge.

For change. For growth. You were built for a wild, rich, spirited, heartfelt, loving, and fascinating ride! Not for frickin' *SAFETY*.

When I say safety, I don't mean seat belts and sunscreen. I don't mean calculated risks or protecting your downside. And I don't mean personal and emotional safety, both of which are essential to our freedom and well-being. The playing it safe I'm talking about is the kind that keeps most people living lives to a fraction of their potential. It's playing small. It's listening to the voice in your head that says, "Who do you think you are to want something more?" It's sometimes delicately—and other times blatantly—hiding from yourself, or perhaps even outright ignoring who you *truly* are and thereby limiting your own greatness. It is what keeps you stuck and betraying yourself—however large or small you measure it—over and over again.

> *Playing it safe with your career looks like staying in a job that's just okay or, even worse, avoiding your dream job, ignoring your true purpose, and never embracing your creativity for fear that you'll be judged as too unrealistic or that what you create won't be seen as valuable.*

> *Playing it safe in relationships looks like allowing the wrong people to gobble up all your time and space and never connecting with the right people—the ones who lift you up and challenge you.*

> *Playing it safe is conformity for no other reason than the fact that well-worn paths seduce us and feel easier because they have been normalized, usually for no reason at all.*

Playing it safe with your heart looks like never being vulnerable, never risking rejection, and missing out on the love you deserve.

Playing it safe in the shadows looks like never being bold enough to stand up and be seen as you truly are.

Ultimately, playing it safe is about fear. And fear is only optimized for survival—not creativity, happiness, joy, connection, harmony, fulfillment, or any of the gifts you have to give or receive in this life.

Because the truth is that the best stuff in life lies just on the other side of your comfort zone. The world will throw you curveballs until you learn to hit them . . . or you quit playing, take your bat, and go home. It cannot "give" you anything, it can only challenge you. Whether you try to meet those challenges, to dance with them in a playful game of discovery and rediscovery, is up to you. Your weaknesses are blessings in that they give you the chance to grow and be brave.

You may have lost sight of this along the way—decades of lying to yourself about what you really want in life, performative behavior designed to avoid friction and fear, and anxiety can do that to you—or you may have even forgotten, but the opposite of playing it safe isn't risk without measure. It's freedom. It's creating the ultimate game in one moment and playing that game the next. It's limitless potential. It's betting on *you.*

At first blush, the idea of seeking discomfort and change without the right tools and proper training can be scary until you realize—actually *remember*—that the tools you need all naturally reside within you right now. Whether you see it or not, you are brave, powerful, and wildly creative at your core. After all, you've made it to this point, haven't you? Your most urgent task, therefore, is to excavate what has been buried deep inside you and learn to use those tools again, because you have much more leverage over your own experience of life than you think. Your task is simply to rediscover how to use these tools.

You don't have to start a revolution. You don't have to quit your job, move to a different country, get a new set of friends, or blow up your life. (Or maybe you do. That's up to you.) But to create the life you want, you *do* have to make a choice between mediocrity and excellence, between what others want for you and what you want for yourself, between fulfilling your potential and hoping that whatever you're doing now will be enough, between playing it safe and playing by your own rules. **This is a book about how to overcome the things that have controlled you in your past and create a life you love. This is the ultimate creative act.**

If you're hesitating while reading this, don't worry. I don't blame you, but it's worth considering why that might be. The good news is that we don't have to go far to find out why:

Your attention has been hijacked.

There's never enough time.

You've been taught to doubt yourself and ignore your intuition.

Constraints have always kept you down.

Play was always second to work.

You were afraid to fail.

And no one ever taught you how to build a practice around what you love most.

Until now. You started down a new path when you picked up this book. These words are for you.

Introduction

Never Play It Safe is about living boldly and understanding the tools that reside naturally within you—right now, wherever you are—such that you can gain, regain, or maintain power over the fear that shows up in your life. This book is not about avoiding mistakes or making your life "perfect." It's about learning to trust yourself and return to your true nature over and over again—each time more quickly and wiser than before. This process is the ultimate creative act for a human being. There are no rules—only experiences that we have and the lessons we can derive from reminding ourselves of who we are and sharing our stories with, and for, one another.

It would be easy to shirk responsibility for wherever we are today in our journey of life, but playing it safe is really more about what we do to ourselves than it is about what the world does to us. We police ourselves to the point of harming our happiness and well-being. We give up because society's idea of success or fulfillment or right or wrong doesn't match our own. Or we stall out, paralyzed. None of it has anything to do with reality or our potential to build a rich or fulfilling life—often it can be as simple and as profound as a lack of awareness and self-knowledge. Paulo Coelho wrote, "Everyone seems to have a clear idea of how other people should lead their lives, but none about his or her own." Truer words.

This is sometimes tough to admit, but the answer to our problems isn't somewhere outside ourselves. We must turn inward for the solution. According to psychologist Dr. Nicole LePera, that revolution is already underway in the form of a wave of increasingly early midlife crises. She sees people in their twenties, thirties, and forties, who played by the rules and followed the plan that society laid out for them asking, "is this all there is?"

That's the tragic part of playing it safe. It's insidious. Like a double agent, we're never sure if we're compromised—until it's clear that we are.

The world shows us a picture of "normal" and then we do the dirty work on ourselves. Whether it's career, relationships, or any other preference for a life we truly long for, we fall into the commonplace trap, crafting a set of seemingly benign, but ultimately self-sabotaging behaviors based on shame, fear, guilt, or another set of emotions we feel for not aligning with the expectations of others. And worse, we begin to tell ourselves—even believe, surreptitiously or otherwise—lies about what we really want from life and what we're truly capable of. Each time, playing it safe starts as a tiny self-betrayal, but just like an explorer who is off by just one degree on her compass, we end up a thousand miles from home.

And to make matters worse, we worry every day about where we are or are not because we have been conditioned by the world to worry.

The silver lining to all of this? It's all bullshit, and it's beatable. We can reverse the damage that's been done. I know because

I've lived both edges of this sword myself, both a victim and a conqueror of playing it safe.

A Willing Concession of Power

The signs started showing up for me in second grade, in Ms. Kelly's class to be exact. I was the proud creator of a weekly comic strip I published and sold at school featuring my leading character Clyde, who looked like a cross between Sasquatch and the ghosts from Pacman, but was a smartass like Garfield; regular magic shows, complete with card tricks, a disappearing scarf, and a top hat; and a stand-up comedy routine where my final joke was always: "What has fifty-two teeth and holds back a monster? . . . My zipper." I honestly had no idea what the punch line meant, but I distinctly remember loving how it made any adult within earshot very nervous and visibly uncomfortable.

So you could say I was a creative, quirky, happy kid, clearly going about my life to the beat of my own drum. Until the day Ms. Kelly told me I shouldn't listen to that drum.

She banned me from selling copies of my comic strip because it was "a business" and therefore wasn't "appropriate" for school. And I received a hefty serving of disapproval for the magic show and the stand-up comedy routines as well. I may have been just eight years old, but surely, I had better things to do, she said to me *and* my parents. So even though I loved the shot of adrenaline I got from getting up in front of an audience and sharing my creative gifts with the world, I gave it all up in an instant. She was not-so-subtly signaling that there was something wrong with the way I was; the sad part was that I immediately began to believe her. Her opinion of what I was meant to be and do mattered more than my own, and I didn't want to be left out in the cold. I was too young and not-at-all prepared to understand that how I spent my time and energy shouldn't really have been up to her.

Foreshadowing be damned.

From that day forward, I stopped standing out and started fitting in. I doubled down on being a jock, and my strategy worked, all the way through high school. I was homecoming royalty, captain of the football and soccer teams, and—surprise—I dated a cheerleader. At the Senior Breakfast, I won the "Typical Senior" award. Whatever that meant, I knew even then it wasn't good. My life was a positively uninspired template for matching the expectations of others. *Typical.*

What I see now is that I was living out of fear—most of which was irrational—and conditioning, for which the French historian and philosopher René Girard had a label: mimesis. According to Girard's thesis, most of us just want the same thing that everyone else wants because it's what we see when we look around. As social animals whose safety and identity once came only from tribes, it's easy to figure out how we ended up here. But once you see and understand mimesis, you can't unsee it. It's everywhere. This is, in part, why we love trailblazers in any industry or walk of life. We notice them and notice other people noticing them, and then, quite simply, we want to *be* them and to be noticed by others ourselves. Evolutionarily, this is true and easy to understand, because it is in being seen by our peers that we are less likely to be at risk of the tribe losing track of us, of being left behind, or of being eaten by a saber-toothed tiger.

The sad truth of this is two-fold. First, mimetic desire is a waste because we are no longer likely to become a meal whilst walking to work. And second, this predicament considers absolutely nothing about what you might truly want for yourself—or be capable of—with this one precious life you've been granted. Thus, a gold mine awaits the handful of us who become aware, break free, figure out what we really want, and remedy this orientation.

I'd like to say that I stumbled on Girard's work in college, grew out of trusting other people's opinions more than my own, and blazed a trail of my own making, but alas, I did not.

Instead I kept letting myself get talked out of living my dreams by people who had given up on theirs. And it became a pattern that I repeated well into adulthood. I'd discover something unique and different about myself that I truly loved—go deep into that thing that made me come alive—and then like clockwork I'd put someone else's idea of what I should be doing above my own. I let myself be pulled toward convention and the illusion of safety again and again. A willing concession of my uniqueness and my power.

In college I traded studies that I loved—art and literature—for premed because it was more impressive when someone asked what I was studying.

I traded a career in professional soccer for medical school at first, and then graduate school later, because I was conditioned to believe it was safer to align around a respectable, well-paying job than make a bet on myself, risking rejection or a blown-out knee.

I even walked away from a dream career as one of the world's top photographers to run a venture-backed startup because it was trendy and because people kept telling me it was the "next logical step in my career." But let's be honest. I also knew my decision would garner near-universal approval from my peers. Looking back, it's clear that although I loved the work and the impact our company made, what played a huge role in my decision to change directions was that founding and building a platform that would be used by millions and would create the possibility of a significant financial exit had the makings of the next great milestone to check off in a life based largely on achievement.

These are just a few of the easiest self-betrayals to describe in a sentence or two. But I made dozens, perhaps hundreds, of other such trade-offs in my careers, relationships, and other areas of my life where I willingly, even if unknowingly, swapped my authentic heart and soul for the tidy, well-worn ruts of others. The reasoning was always the same: either *my dream plan* wasn't reasonable or practical or *I* wasn't.

To be fair, I narrowly managed to navigate my way through, over, and around each of the escapades above, but each came at an exceedingly high cost. Some came with debilitating illnesses due to stress. Others came with $100,000 in student loan debt. Others still resulted in family fights, lost friends, wounded egos, and some serious scar tissue.

All of this suffering on one hand, and yet, on the other, a set of remarkable recoveries. I always bounced back . . . perhaps not in a way I could have anticipated. These, I have come to realize, are the unexpected victories that will ultimately define my life— each allowing for an incrementally healthier, harmonized, and fulfilled chapter beyond the one before it. For example, bailing on medical and graduate school gave me the time to pursue photography full time, and I've earned a hundred times the student debt since then. Leading the startup allowed us to serve tens of millions of students, generate hundreds of millions in revenue, and be acquired by a public company, which provided a financial outcome for the team that made me feel as if the long road was worth the effort in spite of the downside. The family and friends I've bonded with along the way were orders of magnitude more valuable than those I lost, and the bruised ego and scar tissue are what enabled me to take the next step toward *this moment*. I'm much faster now at recognizing the temptation to put my own sense of right and wrong aside in order to do whatever everyone else thinks is best. I'm still not batting a thousand—and I never will be—but I've finally been able to (mostly) short circuit the swing between playing it safe and then needing to course correct.

Hence, this book. We are all in this together.

The Power of a Lever

When Archimedes spoke of a lever long enough to move the world, he was speaking literally. This wasn't madness, courage, or even ego. It was art and science, both a willingness to dream up the impossible and the discipline to follow through on his vision.

When the king heard the mathematician's claim, he asked Archimedes to prove it. How? By moving one of the largest transport ships in the world at the time. This wasn't just any ship. Rumor had it she had only ever completed a single voyage and now sat in the harbor, collecting barnacles. It was a ship so large and stuck that it was believed to be immovable.

So using the principle of leverage, Archimedes got to work and designed an assemblage of tools that he could operate by himself. Then, from the right vantage point, he used those levers and pulleys to fully relocate the ship out of the port and into the sea. One man, fueled by the power of his own creativity, intellect, and a few implements accessible to anyone at the time, was able to single-handedly move a fully loaded sea vessel, including cargo and crew, without even breaking a sweat.

That's the power of leverage.

When the king saw what had happened, he immediately hired Archimedes, who went on to build all kinds of machines that many engineers still marvel at today. What made all this possible was not some incredible resource or gift. It wasn't a lucky break or big idea. It was the right application of the right tool at the right time.

No matter who we are or where we come from, we all deal with what seem like unyielding obstacles in need of a lever—a powerful tool to move them. It's not just external challenges that push us to our limits. Our internal challenges are often even more relentless: we care too much, we won't fit in, we won't be loved, people are counting on us, or we'll fail in public. We imagine that to move our own immovable "ships" and launch ourselves into the lives we dream about, we'd have to figure out some exceedingly complex solution.

But that isn't the case at all.

What I realize in hindsight—and what I hope will resonate with you—is that there are essentially just two modes of being. We are either growing or dying inside, either playing offense or playing defense, in alignment or not, either playing for the love of the game or playing it safe. And in each of these cases, we become aware at some point that if we slow down and listen closely enough, time and again, we can always hear the whisper inside that ultimately leads us back to ourselves.

This—I'm also learning—is how life works. Living cautiously won't save us from missteps or losing ourselves. In fact, the opposite is true. Being too careful keeps us stuck or unfulfilled—or both—because safety is ultimately a mirage. It feels real, possible, reachable, and true, but it is nothing more than a lie. In aiming for a safer, more cautious life, we simply make different missteps and lose ourselves in different— arguably worse—ways. So instead, our goal must be to live boldly, make mistakes, and then to use the tools that are naturally alive within us to learn and recover quickly. We don't need to beat ourselves up or give up on where we were meant to go; we simply have to learn to trust that we *can and will* right the ship. This insanely practical sort of wisdom is what I promise to share with you in this book: the knowledge that you are extraordinarily capable, and it's time that you lean into the courage to rely on this.

As such, when it comes to breaking through the difficult things in your own life—or even building a life you previously thought to be impossible—you must remember that you have the same power of Archimedes's lever within you, only instead of moving *the* world, you can move *your* world. The process doesn't start with chasing the latest fad or life hack, or wrangling the best education, job, relationship, or anything external. The job is an inside one, and so it begins with you.

Levers for Life

It's often said that your specific combination of DNA, your life experiences from childhood up till now, is one of a kind, and that the person you are is somewhere on the order of 1 in 400 trillion. Thus, the odds are long that there has ever been another one of you before nor will there be another you anytime soon.

Regardless of whether the math is accurate, the idea is seductive: you are one of a kind. And yet it seems that this notion somehow paralyzes us instead of emboldening us. Rather than being inspired to make meaning and create a masterpiece from our one precious life, we get talked out of it in an innocuous, almost innocent way. Then we're left without the benefits that come along with a life full of purpose. As a result, we end up conditioned to shape our strengths and interests to fit society, rather than leveraging them into an extraordinary life that's driven by both a rich, human experience and the ability to make the world a better place.

But I'm guessing you know people who have bucked this conditioned pattern. You can just feel it when you're with them because they somehow seem more alive. And my god what a special type of charisma that is. It's magnetic.

Throughout this book, there are dozens—maybe hundreds—of examples of people like this. Some you may have heard of before, while others will be completely new. The caution that I offer is that while the book shares the stories of people who have done extraordinary *things—that is to say created extraordinary outcomes*—I would urge you to not focus on the outcomes themselves. "I think everybody should get rich and famous and do everything they ever dreamed of so they can see that it's not the answer," said Jim Carrey, and he's right. It's not about fame or money or the car you're driving or awards or any other validation from the outside world. All of us have magic inside us, no matter if we're introverts or extroverts, no matter our shape, size, orientation, color, or background. We are all ordinary people remembering that we have a capacity for an extraordinary life in every sense of the word.

I can't help but think of *The Wizard of Oz*. What we remember from the movie is Dorothy closing her eyes, clicking her heels together three times, and saying, "there's no place like home." But equally important is what Glinda says to Dorothy right before that when the Wizard is not able to help her. "You don't need to be helped any longer," the Good Witch says. "You've always had the power to go back to Kansas." When Dorothy asks why no one ever told her, Glinda reminds her that she had to uncover the truth for herself to know for sure she had this power inside. The same is true for you. So let's focus on the resources you've got inside you and the practical ways you can reveal and put your very own mojo to work. The external outcomes you seek—and who am I to decide or judge them—are only possible as a downstream effect of looking inside, rediscovering who you are, and using the innate tools within you.

In this book, I share everything I know about these tools, why we get talked out of trusting them (and ourselves), and how to rediscover our natural power . . . all in the name of creating a life worth loving. This is not an easy life per se— there's no such thing as effortless brilliance—but a life built on these principles is one where you get to write your own story instead of living the one the world is trying to sell you.

On this journey, I'll illustrate just how to do this by sharing strategies and ideas from some of the world's most interesting humans, along with my own lessons and insights.

The goal is not to tell you to live like this person or that one, or to follow someone else's path. Rather, the idea is to get you imagining what just might be possible, just like Archimedes, by using simple, well-directed inputs to yield massive outputs.

In my experience, there are seven basic levers for life but thousands of ways to combine them. Each chapter in this book focuses on one of these tools or "levers" that will help you get more of what you want from what you already have. How you do that is up to you and will be unique to your particular journey. Here's a brief summary of each lever for life:

- **Attention**—Your human superpower, and the first step toward a life you love, requires that you learn to skillfully direct your attention and keep distractions at bay. Your experience of life is what you focus on, and all of this can be entirely of your choosing.

- **Time**—Despite what we've been told, time is not some uniform conveyor belt moving us closer to our death every day. You've had the experience of time expanding and contracting based on what you're doing, how you're doing it, and who you're with. Flow states and all the time to do as you choose are readily available and well within your reach.

- **Intuition**—Trusting your gut is the most valuable tool you've been taught to ignore. Until now. Get

ready to burn the standard-issue map to success
(whatever that means) and instead to live by your
own inner compass.

• **Constraints**—The world places limits on us, but it's
the limits and constraints we apply to our own lives
that give us a massive advantage when it comes to
unlocking a bold and creative life. In many cases,
you'll learn to leverage the very thing that's been
holding you back.

• **Play**—It's not board games, glue sticks, and
glitter, and it's definitely not just for kids. Relish
in remembering that play is the engine of life.
Recapture the joy and energy in everything you do
to drive better outcomes and put everything into a
broader perspective.

• **Failure**—It's time you completely reimagine failure
as a stepping-stone to success. This isn't a trite
phrase with a pot of gold at the end of the rainbow.
Life isn't about avoiding mistakes—it's about
recovering quickly and learning to trust yourself
again and again.

• **Practice**—The sum of all these parts: practice is
the art of consistent action. Thinking about what
you want is not enough. The actions that make up
your days will shape your life into what it ultimately
becomes, so what and how you practice matters.

While I don't want to be overly prescriptive, I recommend reading the book all the way through on your first pass, over-indexing on the most critical individual levers. Focus on what excites or inspires you the most such that you can reconnect with yourself and your desires, and reset your expectations of yourself and your life. Whether you choose to engage first with what feels most challenging or most accessible, that's up to you, but either way, as you learn to use each of the levers in turn, you'll be increasingly able to see how everything fits together, and you'll find helpful nuggets of wisdom in every single one of the chapters.

While some of the changes you make will feel like a weight lifted from your shoulders, not everything you learn and do here at first will register as "fun." For example, creating constraints for yourself may not initially seem joyful ("I want it ALL!" you're thinking), but learning how to limit your exposure to the toxic traits of others might create just enough space in your life so that you can find the freedom to fail. Or the fact that Practice sounds a lot like work may seem intimidating *until* you see that the chapter is chock-full of insights about building small, easy habits that are key to the life you're seeking.

From that point, you can use *Never Play It Safe* as a reference guide whenever you want to level up or you're feeling stuck. Need to remember how to trust yourself again? The section on Intuition will re-ground you and get you back on track. Spending too much time staring into your phone? Review the Attention chapter. Or when life feels too heavy and you've lost its meaning or its measure, Play is always there for you.

My goal isn't to offer a one-size-fits-all blueprint but rather an indication of what might be possible. Ultimately, a person's life is whatever they make it. We each can stay stuck in our old patterns of living and being, following the rulebooks given to us by others, or we can dare to build something of our own design. In the end, it's my hope that you'll use this book not to reveal how life is—but how it could be for you. Something you love.

An Example to Revere

Why the hell is Brandon calling me at five o'clock in the morning?

"Hey, man," I said, half-asleep, blinking through bleary eyes as I rolled out of bed. I looked out the window. The sun wasn't even up yet. "Are you okay? What's going on?"

It was 5:05 a.m. in Seattle. As a native east coaster and a world traveler, it wasn't the first time in our long-standing friendship that Brandon had forgotten about those things called time zones, but it was endearing, and I loved him for it.

"Yo!" he said, full of energy and life. "I'm standing in the town square here in Accra, Ghana, and there's this kid. He stops me, says he knows me from your podcast . . . and CreativeLive. Says his dream is to transform photography in Africa."

The "kid's" name was Paul Ninson. Several years before, at twenty years old, he and his girlfriend had had a baby out of wedlock. Because of deeply rooted cultural beliefs, Paul felt like his life was over for the shame the baby brought on both of their families. Coming from a poor family, he had no money and no obvious way to support his daughter, but he spent every minute he wasn't in school hustling and trying to provide. At first, he printed and sold t-shirts, but when he saw a friend make more in a few hours from photographing a wedding than he made selling a hundred shirts, he decided he needed to get a camera and learn photography for himself.

By the time he approached Brandon, Paul had been listening to my podcast for years and was an avid student of CreativeLive, an online learning platform for creators and entrepreneurs that I'd started seven or eight years before, which was being used by millions of people across 170 countries. I didn't know it at the time, but Paul had become so obsessed with photography, so convinced of its power and potential to improve his life, that he'd given up his apartment and sold all his possessions—including his phone—to scrape together enough money for his first proper camera. He was committed to taking photos every day, training his attention to see the world in a new way. And he was imagining a future in which he could give up photographing events and instead earn a living as an African photographer telling African stories.

In spite of not having any money, he kept trying to put himself in the right places to grow, learn, and connect with other working artists. At one point, he traveled from his village to a meeting of "professional" photographers in the capital of Accra, only to be turned away at the gate for his cheap camera and for not having a body of work. He was crushed, but instead of giving up, Paul kept learning and honing his craft. He was so determined that he eventually spent six hundred dollars, all the money he had at the time, to fly to Kenya for a documentary project about a community of women he'd read about who had built a small town to escape their abusive husbands. When the project was finished, Paul celebrated. Finally, he had a story he could sell to magazines and websites, but after countless emails and cold calls, no one was interested.

Paul felt like he had failed.

But the Brandon that Paul spotted that fateful day in the town square in Accra happened to be the artist behind *Humans of New York*, one of the most impressive, ambitious—and successful—photography projects in modern history. Paul sensed a chance to receive meaningful feedback on his work from a true, uber-successful artist working at the height of his craft. But what began as a chance for Paul to learn from Brandon turned into something more. Brandon, as he often does when meeting strangers, turned the tables on Paul and began to ask him questions about his life and how he had started taking pictures. Eventually Paul showed Brandon the photos from Kenya—the portfolio he had prepared as a downstream effect of previous rejections implying that he wasn't an *actual* photographer—that he now carried with him literally everywhere he went. Brandon immediately recognized the quality of the work, the honesty and integrity of the images, and the emotion Paul had captured with his camera. Each portfolio image felt like an entire story captured in a single frame. Brandon was stunned by Paul's work as well as by how much Paul had accomplished in spite of how few resources had been available to him up to that point.

As for Paul, in the wake of that seemingly random rendezvous on the street with one of his creative heroes, he was intuitively aware of the connection he'd made, but he was reluctant to get too emotionally invested in any future outcome. He'd been burned by "the industry" before, told time and again that his dream to become a photographer was a fool's errand.

When Brandon returned from Africa, we got together to talk about his trip and his incredible meeting with Paul. Over dinner that night, he relayed to me that Paul had applied to the International Center of Photography's prestigious program and that, although Paul had received both the Director's Fellowship and a George Moss Merit Scholarship, it was impossible for him to afford even the partial tuition that remained beyond the stipends. Because of this financial barrier, Paul's application acceptance had lapsed.

I could tell from the look in Brandon's eyes and the tone of his voice that he had a plan up his sleeve. *What if we—as established pros familiar with Paul's work—could somehow help him reactivate his acceptance to the program?* And could we perhaps help offset the tuition gap and maybe even hire him for some work? A plan was hatched.

With Paul's permission, we took to writing letters of recommendation to the ICP asking them to reinstate Paul's admission. Miraculously, the plan worked. Between the scholarships and a small stipend Brandon paid Paul to help him on a series he was filming, Paul could finally move to New York and live his dream of enrolling in a formal photography program and getting to work on his purpose.

This was Paul's season of practice, of putting in the hours to get the most out of his education. He worked around the clock, splitting his time between going to school, studying on his own, and working with Brandon, watching a master in action, telling people's stories on the streets of New York. His attention was completely trained on living his dream, and it was the perfect apprenticeship. Paul's favorite study location was the New York Public Library—which he visited every day without fail, awestruck by the collection of knowledge. "This place had every book in the world," he said, especially amazed by the books he found that were full of photographs from Ghana. "When I was learning to be a photographer, these books could have helped me so much." He also went around the city to secondhand bookstores, buying any books on African photography he could find.

Most of the money he made from working with Brandon was sent back home to his daughter in Africa. Whatever was left was spent almost entirely on the books from which he'd learned photography and had grown to love. Paul was leveraging all of the opportunities that were available to him so that he could learn, grow, and build a life that everyone he knew, including himself, once thought was impossible.

His time in New York was not without challenges, however, and they weren't only financial in nature. As a foreigner and a person of color he was routinely—both at school and while training as a photojournalist—subjected to racism. Some people wouldn't shake his hand, while others would shout in his face to "go home" to Africa. He was even handed money on the subway while on his way to work and told to "buy some food."

And yet Paul pressed on.

Then, on the cusp of his completing the ICP program—as if he'd written his very own script for his life—the world seemingly cracked open for him. One prestigious, well-paying photography job led to another and seemingly overnight he was earning a living like he'd always imagined—one previously thought to be out of reach back in Accra. With ample funds to send home in support of his daughter Ella, an increasing volume of commercial work on the horizon, and a production role supporting

Brandon, his life—and more importantly his growing awareness of what was possible—had reached a completely new level.

Time and time again, Paul could have given up, he could have played it safe, letting the suffering, the friction in his life, and his fear get the better of him. Instead, he focused his attention and time on learning his craft through deliberate practice, and faced down the financial, cultural, and geographical constraints that threatened his idea of what he wanted his life to be. By all accounts, his own and that of the world around him, Paul had become a smashing success. With the tools he had learned to use, he was ready to continue building the bold, creative life he had imagined when he'd fallen in love with photography in Ghana years before.

As the saying goes, "We have two lives, and the second begins when we realize we have only one." Paul's second life had officially begun—and with this book, so perhaps has yours.

Lever 1

Attention

The Superpower

From the moment we're born, we must get attention or die.

Babies are survival machines. Every coo, every cry, every attempt at eye contact—those tiny people have to grab our attention or game over. The way they settle into our arms and sigh . . . the message is clear. "Feed me! Hold me! Sing to me! Love me!" And when we respond, they grow, they thrive, they connect with us . . . and then with others for a lifetime.

But when a baby doesn't receive sufficient touch and connection from a parent or caregiver, even when they're getting proper nutrition, they struggle to make it through the first phase of life. Remember the Romanian orphanages of the 1980s and 1990s, full of thousands of abandoned children warehoused in sterile hospital wards? Sure, these babies received food and some medical care, all assembly-line style, but no one ever held them or soothed them. They lay alone in their cribs for months and years, and most never learned to walk or talk. Without care and attention as babies and toddlers, they were condemned to a lifetime of health problems and severe attachment disorder if they even made it out of the orphanage at all. Sadly, many died from neglect.

But it's not just kids who are attention-seeking missiles. The world is exploding with adults who demand our attention at work, at home, and online. Actually—who am I kidding? We've *all* been there before. We spend a ridiculous amount of time and energy screaming into the void, "Look at me!" in an attempt to get love, praise, friends, likes, or followers. At every age and across nearly every cultural paradigm, our primal instinct to seek attention is on display 24/7. We're conditioned to believe there is no other way. Getting attention is how a person stands out, makes a difference, finds a mate, gets a promotion, builds a business, and connects with others.

Getting attention is everything in this life.

But what if I told you that nearly everything you've been taught about attention is wrong? That as an adult it is precisely the *seeking* of attention that keeps you trapped, stuck, and playing it safe?

We've seen this play out way too often: the kid who was popular in high school, talked loud and fast, and made off-color jokes finds himself later in life jockeying for the big job, hoping to get the gig to feel whole again, even if just for a week or two. Or the parent who lives through the accomplishments of their child—pushing them to be a doctor, a lawyer, an engineer, or whatever the high-status flavor of the month is just so that everyone will tell them what a good mom or dad they are.

Think about the billionaire geek who buys an entire social

network, so he can funnel millions of eyeballs to himself every day of the week.

Or the "influencer." Look at what I had for breakfast!

It's an endless loop—seeking attention, getting some; seeking more attention, different attention, getting it; and so on and so forth into infinity. Because at the end of the day, we always want MORE, whether we're fueling our egos or our biological needs. As a species, humans are social animals.

But what if there's a better way?

What if, instead of constantly trying to *get* attention from others, you did a 180 and spent all that energy learning to *direct* your attention? What if you became mindful and aware? Narrowed your focus and *strengthened* your ability to be in the now? What if you were able to tackle the tasks right in front of you without losing sight of the ones in the distance that will eventually fulfill your goals and dreams? What if you were able to listen—really listen—to the people whom you love or who interest you? If you weren't processing what you were about to say while they were speaking, and you were entirely present with their words, ideas, and emotions? What if you could—just by using your attention effectively—send a clear and powerful message to everyone in your presence that you truly see and hear them?

Talk about a transformation.

By extension, what if you were also ruthless with distractions and could ignore them with ease? Not just your phone, but news that doesn't serve you, the boss who's lost his mind, the mistake you made at dinner last night, and the annoying traffic during your commute. What if turning off all the noise—literally and figuratively—was as easy for you as brushing your teeth, or any other habit you've developed? What if you were so good at directing your attention that you were squarely in the driver's seat for all the controllable aspects of your life?

In this day and age, we've become willing participants in haphazardly doling out attention to anything and everything. After all, we never *really* have to decide what to focus on. Hop online and an algorithm hijacks your brain until you "wake up," only to discover that hours have passed with nothing much to show for it. We know we need to turn away from the screens, get outside, connect with other humans, and sleep, yet the fear of missing out on the next news cycle, meme, trend, or viral video has us checking our phones 144 times per day. If your attention is a sleek pane of glass, then technology shatters it into a million little pieces.

But before we blame the wizards designing the masterful UX that keeps us hooked, it's incumbent upon us to acknowledge our own complicity. When it comes to attention, we play it safe by amusing ourselves to death, staying distracted, and refusing to unplug from the constant onslaught of images and information. To be fair, the scientists who study this phenomenon have warned that it's a vicious cycle: using technology to soothe our anxiety only ends up causing new, more, and different kinds of anxiety. So when it comes to living a life by design rather than by default, we have to *decide* to step out of the technological fray in order to carve our way through the algorithmic land mines, face ourselves, and figure out what we really want.

I'm just doing what everyone else does, you might be saying. *This is the norm now. Don't be so out of step.*

But that is now precisely your new goal. If "out-of-step"

means living an intentional life in which you actively choose what to focus on and how to chart your own course in a way that feels as natural and unforced as breathing, then I bet you'd take a double serving.

Consider training your attention the first step toward the rest of your life. To become so out of step that you stop mindlessly giving away your attention and instead reclaim the most precious resource you have. Trust that only when you begin to make that break can you finally bask in the beauty of the unmediated experience of the world and yourself.

Dr. Andrew Huberman, associate professor of neurobiology and ophthalmology at Stanford University School of Medicine, says boldly that the ability to focus and direct attention "is *the* distinguishing factor between those who will succeed in any endeavor and those who won't."

Read that again. *The* factor for success in *any* endeavor.

Therefore, let's be crystal clear that it's not an overstatement to say that in order to be a happy, healthy, and fulfilled human being—to be your best or get unstuck from any situation now or in the future—you must recognize attention for the superpower it really is and learn to train it on the parts of your life that matter most. This is the most urgent task before you, and it's entirely doable with a little direction and reasonable effort. Let's get started.

Attention as Life Force

When the Nazis invaded Austria in 1938, psychiatrist Viktor Frankl could have escaped, but he refused to leave his parents to die. Four difficult years later, in 1942, he and his entire family were deported to Theresienstadt, where his father died from starvation and pneumonia. Then, in 1944, the rest of the family was transferred to Auschwitz, where Frankl's mother and brother were sent to the gas chambers. Frankl's wife later died in Bergen-Belsen.

A different person would have given up entirely, might have even gone willingly to join his loved ones in death rather than enduring years of watching the suffering and torture all around him. Instead, Frankl focused his attention on treating suicidal patients in the camps and set up a suicide prevention group. Prior to the war, he had treated thousands of suicidal women at Steinhof Psychiatric Hospital, and now he focused his attention on work that had mattered to him before the war and that continued to matter to him in spite of the horror all around him.

When Frankl returned to Vienna after the war, the sophisticated, cultured world of the Ringstrasse had vanished, but he set to work rewriting a book on his therapeutic methods, the original manuscript, which had been taken from him at Theresienstadt. At first he devoted just one chapter to his time in the camps, but when his publisher asked him to expand that chapter, he wrote *Man's Search for Meaning* during a feverish nine-day period. Published anonymously in 1946, it went on to become one of the most influential books of all time and the most famous of the thirty-nine books Frankl published during his career.

Frankl understood the power of attention in a way that transcends words. Among his many insights, he writes, "Everything can be taken from a man but one thing: the last of the human freedoms—to choose one's attitude in any given set of circumstances, to choose one's own way." Even under the worst of circumstances, Frankl found ways to choose what he would focus on—in his case purpose—as a way to stave off the darkness of his circumstances. He spent the rest of his life fighting against what he called the "existential vacuum" of modern life and trying to connect people with their own sense of agency and intention. Talk about a mission that's still relevant today, one that many people would even argue is the meaning of life.

Like Frankl, the psychologist Mihaly Csikszentmihalyi also used the power of his attention to survive World War II. As a prisoner in an Italian work camp, he connected with the idea of flow for which he has become famous. How did he achieve such a unique, enlightened, and effortless state in which the world faded away and the only thing left was the task right in front of him? By playing chess. Using a game of strategy as a way to turn his attention inward—away from the atrocities around him—he was able to fully immerse himself in an activity that not only challenged him but helped him grow. As a result, he fared far better than most of his peers.

There's also Louis Zamperini, whose story was told in the bestselling book and film, *Unbroken*. An Olympic runner turned World War II bombardier, Zamperini was captured by the Japanese after a plane crash left him adrift for 47 days in the Pacific Ocean. His survival hinged on where he directed his attention, so he focused on maintaining his mental strength, even during prolonged torture. His attention not only sustained him but became the driving force behind the faith and forgiveness that defined his postwar life.

Few of us will ever be faced with the atrocities and horror

that Frankl, Csikszentmihalyi, and Zamperini experienced, but all of us can learn from them. In the most dire circumstances, a focus on resilience, forgiveness, connection, or the future not only saved these men's lives and powerfully supported those around them, but it also enabled their postwar healing and re-demption. Their stories are a testament to the transformative power of attention and a reminder to all of us that it is one of the greatest powers in the universe.

A Light in the Darkness

Consider the flashlight.

We switch it on, and, like magic, a beam of light illuminates a circle right in front of us. Outside that circle is darkness—we have no idea what's going on out there—but within the circle, we can see the finest details: blades of grass, a lost glove, a trail, or anything else within that glowing circumference. When we move forward, the beam of light shows us where to go even if we occasionally have to backtrack through the darkness. But the light of the flashlight allows us to examine what's right in front of us and lets everything else fade to black.

Attention works much the same way. When we train the beam of our attention on something, we see it and ourselves much more clearly. Contrary to popular opinion, where we choose to place our attention is something that is almost 100 percent within our control. Yet, most of us don't live this way.

We *think* we have good days and bad days, that there is good weather and bad weather, that we encounter nice people and mean people—all of which affect us in some way. But we don't really *have* any of those things. What we have—all that we have, in fact—is our attention. As psychologist William James wrote over a hundred years ago: "My experience is what I agree to attend to."

If we're trying to attend to everything, if our attention is fractured into a million little pieces, we ultimately aren't able to attend to anything. In the attention economy, attention is as valuable as housing, food, water, and money. And yet we spend our attention carelessly without realizing it's the most important resource we have.

Because, for better or worse, what we pay attention to expands.

Have you ever obsessively followed a news story only to find out that your office mate or your mom has no idea what you're talking about? Or maybe you had a disagreement with a friend twenty years ago, but when you apologize, your friend doesn't even remember that it happened? On the flip side, maybe you do a thirty-day gratitude experiment and almost immediately feel a greater sense of well-being. Perhaps you focus ten minutes every morning on writing a paragraph of your novel, and after two months, you have fifty pages. With the power of our attention, we can dictate the direction and the quality of our lives.

Paying attention is everything in this life.

What this means for us as a species—or rather YOU—is profound. You can get swept away by petty aggravations or news or what everyone else tells you is important, *or* you can decide for yourself what the building blocks of your life will be. Much of what you casually pay attention to depletes you or dims your light, but when you decide, *actually choose*, where to focus, you can begin to make things, build things, create things, and that momentum will carry you toward a new life in which you can jettison the BS and spend your days engaged in work and relationships that bring meaning, purpose, and joy to your life and the lives of others close to you.

As you become more aware of what you pay attention to, you will start to see how much your mind is making up the world you're living in. And that's the moment you can really start to change things. It's not easy, but when we change what we notice, when we *choose* what we focus on rather than relying on chance or worse, everything changes.

Shutting Out the World

It's not enough to train our attention on what matters. We must also protect it as if our life depended on it. *Because it does*.

Distractions take two distinct forms. External distractions like a pinging phone, task-switching all day long, or toxic, one-sided relationships not only keep us from accomplishing our greatest goals, they erode our ability to pay attention at all. Often we don't even see these disturbances and interruptions as unusual—so many people live busy, chaotic, emotionally amped-up lives—but it's only because we've forgotten that fracturing our attention is not how we're meant to live. We've forgotten the peace and joy that come from focusing on something we love, and we view the pursuit of these emotions as self-indulgent.

But even when we get away from our phones and computers, we still have to deal with the second, and perhaps even more difficult form of distraction: internal distraction. Ask anyone, and they can describe a persistent stream of thoughts running through their minds. *Did I turn off the stove before I left the house?*

How am I going to make rent this month? Have we missed our chance to save the planet and slow global warming? In the midst of this near-constant swirl of thoughts and existential worry, we've forgotten that our natural state is deep attention. Constantly jumping from idea to idea or task to task is actually *not* how humans were meant to live.

Yet we insist on distracting ourselves from ourselves because it can be easier than sitting in silence and facing the truth about who we really are or what we really want. Whether this kind of quiet and stillness is part of a ten-day Vipassana meditation retreat or simply a moment of calm in the midst of a frenetic life, it can be maddening when we strip away all the crap and are left alone with our own desires and disappointments. Alas, there is no other way to start to pay attention to our lives and to what comes next.

Though it takes time, practice, and determination, it is possible both to train ourselves to focus on what matters most *and* ignore what drains or doesn't serve us. Then and only then will we be in a position to stop reacting out of habit and conditioning and start having a choice about how we show up and respond to our world.

Do you want more freedom?

Do you want an exceptional existence, one worthy of your potential?

Start by learning to skillfully direct and protect your attention—and prepare to move mountains.

We Become What We Behold

So how do we transform from moving through the world unconsciously, letting our minds skip from subject to subject without much awareness to being able to use attention to our advantage? In my own case, it happened during the first year when I decided to become a photographer.

Kate and I were living in a tiny apartment, and I was working in a ski shop to make ends meet. There were a lot of voices in my head telling me how I had screwed up the familiar patterns of school and job; plus, I had a boatload of doubt, no money, and few role models. Even though I whispered to those closest to me that I wanted to be a photographer, I was too scattered—and too scared—to actually pay attention to what I might have to do to make that dream a reality.

I spent the first few months of that time dabbling, working in the shop, explaining myself to everyone I knew, and trying, but failing, to hone my craft. My attention was too fractured to get anywhere, but at a certain point, it was do or die. Yes, I had to earn a living, but more importantly, that rare, humble, honest version of myself that sometimes showed up on morning walks or while gazing at golden-orange sunsets had a point: I had to stop fucking around and making excuses. I had to stop paying so much attention to the toxic voices in my head telling me I'd never make it as a photographer and instead go all in on the next right step that would get me where I wanted to go.

And so I went to the library.

I loved photography, but I didn't know how to make the leap from amateur photographer to full-time artist. Today my life is full of people living bold, creative lives, but a couple of decades ago, I was one of just a handful of people I knew who had stepped off a traditional path, and I had almost no real-life examples of how to do what I wanted to do. So rather than keep my attention focused on all the naysayers, I began—ever so incrementally—by focusing on what might be possible.

I couldn't afford the time or money it would have taken to go to art school, so I jump-started my creative education by reading artist autobiographies and watching documentaries about Basquiat, Rauschenberg, Patti Smith, and the Velvet Underground—I devoured anything about the New York City art scene. I went to museums and art exhibits. And I latched on to Andy Warhol's advice to artists or anyone building a creative life: "Don't think about making art, just get it done. Let everyone else decide if it's good or bad, whether they love it or hate it. While they are deciding, make even more art."

Immersing myself in the stories of artists before me who hadn't played it safe allowed me to focus on what it meant to live this life—the benefits and the pitfalls. I wasn't the first person to go on this journey, so I stopped being so precious and careful, and from there I was able to step into the flow of my attention without the constant distraction of self-doubt. That permission slip freed me up. Instead of paying so much attention to what I was leaving behind, I could focus on where I was going and how others like me had gotten there.

I spent hours in the stacks, pulling out book after book and reading with rapt attention. I took many of the volumes home to reread them to myself and to Kate, who was far less concerned with traditional markers of success than I was and who saw the possibilities even before I did. And I started to know myself and realize that when I got quiet, I had more self-knowledge inside me than I had given myself credit for.

From there, focusing my attention became easier. My friends and I were all in our twenties—they had their first real jobs and were spending money on restaurants, cars, and condos. But I didn't have that kind of money—or any discretionary funds to speak of—so I stopped going out. I needed to focus my attention and everything I was earning on learning to be a photographer. Otherwise I wasn't going to make it. I spent hundreds of Friday and Saturday nights after that developing film in my bathroom-turned-darkroom.

And I didn't mind at all. This is one of the side effects of not playing it safe: when you stop trying to do what everyone else is doing and start experimenting in order to discover what you truly care deeply about, your ability to focus becomes greatly amplified. This is one secret of the people living their dreams. There's a virtuous cycle at work: focused attention on what you love, in turn, creates more focused attention.

Like anything, this is a continual process of improvement, but as with all the levers in this book, the objective has never been perfection. It's momentum. My goal has simply been to keep my ability to focus active enough so that even if I have the occasional setback, I can always return to a place in which I have a choice of what to focus on and what to ignore. I would never equate my experience to Frankl's, Csikszentmihalyi's, or Zamperini's, but I am saying that whether we like it or not, whether we want it or not, we all face a crossroads at some point when we have to decide to use our attention in the first step toward living the way we want to live.

My version of refusing to play it safe with my career was training my attention on my craft and the process of photography. I wanted to be an artist and entrepreneur even though everyone around me was skeptical. And sure, I floundered at the beginning. Everyone does. But the repeated process of directing and protecting my attention was a force multiplier that contributed to my progress. I couldn't be what I couldn't see, so training myself to see and believe in my own potential through the experiences of other artists was a key step and the first of many breakthroughs. I've come back to "paying attention" as a strategy over and over again, quite simply because it is the most foundational tool in our kit. That's why attention is the first lever in this book.

May I Direct Your Attention?

The world is largely out of our control, so managing our attention begins with addressing what we *can* control. Internal distractions are often just as—or more—powerful than external ones, so before we move ahead, let's figure out how to deal with the self-sabotaging thoughts and feelings that most often keep us stuck, fearful, and playing it safe.

Crashing through the jungle of our own minds can be complicated, but if we can see our own thoughts and feelings in a neutral, nonjudgmental way, we can separate them from who we are as people. That perspective gives us freedom to respond to what comes our way without any preconceived notions or judgments. "You have power over your mind—not outside events," wrote Marcus Aurelius almost two thousand years ago. "Realize this and you will find strength."

You Are Not Your Thoughts

How we feel is not as automatic as we often assume.

The first step in using your attention as a lever is understanding that what you think and believe is not who you are. Yes, emotions are a part of our lives. But how we feel springs from what we allow ourselves to focus on. We might get bad news and have to move through uncomfortable feelings, but you can learn to not be controlled by those emotions. Consider, for example, what happens when someone says something rude to you, and you take it personally.

There are 86,400 seconds in a day, and maybe the insult lasted 5 seconds or even 25. Should the tiniest fraction of the day absorb all of our attention? Obviously not, but how many times do we dwell on these kinds of comments and spend the rest of the day rehearsing what we *could* have said without really feeling any better? Or worse, using those five seconds as the basis for a "bad day"?

I learned early about the power of choice when it comes to focusing—or not—on the negative. When I was in middle school, my father took me to a seminar on sports psychology. When it came time for a demonstration, the psychologist leading the seminar called me to the stage and asked me to close my eyes and hold my arm straight out in front of me at shoulder level as she performed a hypnosis of sorts on me. She told me to imagine that someone had wronged me, and then said that it just so happened that I had a chance for revenge as I was about to compete directly against this person in a sporting event.

"How does that feel in your body?" she asked.

"I feel angry, aggressive, strong, and powerful," I responded.

She asked me to picture my revenge, besting my competition

in every way imaginable. As I created a vision of the outcome she had described in my mind, she used her own strength and body weight to pull my arm back down to my side. I stood there, fighting against gravity and her weight as she slowly managed to pull it back alongside my body. "Very impressive," she said. "That's real power."

In the second scenario, the psychologist guided me to think about the most beautiful thing I could imagine. Favorite friends, pets I loved, the feeling in my body of winning the state championship in soccer, or being named MVP of a tournament. Again, I extended my arm in front of me parallel to the stage floor. But this time, she was not able to move my arm from its parallel position, and although she was smaller in stature, she was able to literally hang off my arm for a brief moment in what was the equivalent of more than a hundred-pound lateral raise with one arm, a feat that anyone who has spent time in a weight room knows is exceedingly difficult for a world class bodybuilder, let alone a lanky teenager.

The final element of my experience, before returning me from a hypnotic state, was her suggestion to my subconscious that I would be able to remember the experience in great detail, from the feelings in my body to the distinction in the power between my positive and negative emotions, and be able to extend this experience beyond sports to other areas of my life. This became an insight for me and was a powerful force in shaping my future.

To this day I recall these events with a bit of awe. How is it that a silly demonstration from decades ago can have such a profound effect on me both in the moment and to this day? It's because it made me imagine what results could be possible by simply training this ability and kicked off a lifelong fascination for me around the power of attention.

The fact is that you, too, have more of a choice of how to respond in that situation than you may be giving yourself credit for. That's not to say other people won't behave badly sometimes or there aren't scars from your past that don't sometimes take hold of the present, but when you stop ruminating, or focusing solely on what hurts, bothers, or annoys you—or better yet allow yourself to experience those emotions in a non-judgmental way and then consciously decide to move on—you can begin to heal, whether from the inconvenience of the person who cut you off on your commute, or from some of life's more substantial challenges.

You Are Not What Happens to You

There's an old story about a Chinese farmer. One day, the farmer's horse gets out of the stable and runs away, and all the villagers say to him, "Isn't it horrible that your horse got out?"

The farmer responds, "Good news, bad news. Who knows?"

The next day, the horse returns with four more wild horses. Now the farmer has five horses. The village people say, "Wow! Isn't that amazing? Your horse brought back four horses! You are so lucky!"

But the farmer simply replies, "Good news, bad news. Who knows?"

Then the farmer's son is trying to tame the wild horses and gets bucked off. He breaks his leg. The villagers tell him, "Isn't it horrible that your son broke his leg?"

The farmer says, "Good news, bad news. Who knows?"

The next day, the military comes and takes all able-bodied

boys to serve in the army—except for the farmer's son, because his leg is broken. He can't go to war due to his injury, and the villagers say, "How lucky are you?"

The farmer says, "Good news, bad news. Who knows?"

And on and on it goes. The farmer experiences life as it is happening instead of placing judgments and expectations on it. His perspective is one of openness and flexibility. Nothing is good or bad to him—it's just happening. He is aware of the events in his life but decides to remain neutral. This mindset results in a belief that shapes his reality. And as a result, he is free from attachment and can live life as it comes.

With practice, we can do the same.

Some may call certain experiences "good," and others may call them "bad." But in the end, those are just judgments about the experiences. How you think about the events in your life is your call and ultimately what determines their goodness or badness. The weather is just being weather. The traffic is just being traffic, and bad things happen to good people. In the words of the band Dawes, "Things happen—that's all they ever do."

The true measure of a life boils down to what consumes your attention, and even though it might not always feel like it, you get to decide what that is. Learning to direct your attention is a bit of a magic wand for helping you move from a reactive life to an intentional one—which is the only place from which you can change anything.

Train It and Trust It

Before we can see the world as it is, we must understand how much of it is a projection of our internal state. With this in mind, sports psychologist Bob Rotella references a concept he calls "train it and trust it." In his book *Golf Is Not a Game of Perfect*, he shares how most golfers only trust their swings when they're playing well. But as soon as things start going poorly, they stop believing in themselves. As a result of this judgment, reactivity, and ensuing lack of confidence, their performance declines. "When great athletes stop trusting," he writes, "they stop being great."

The same is true for us. The world is largely neutral in nature, so why should we project instead of remaining neutral? The answer is, of course, that we are emotionally rich creatures, bathed in our neurology and biochemistry; therefore, it makes no sense that we are so quick to falter and give away our attention—our power in any moment—so easily when we can train ourselves to behave otherwise.

Thus, any daily practice (see the sidebar below for some options) that trains us to create even the tiniest space between stimulus and response helps remind us to let our attention be the guide rather than our feelings. Instead of "I am angry," you can remind yourself, "I am experiencing anger," or rather than "I am happy," you might say, "I am experiencing joy." Emotions can be powerful, but they are also fleeting, like clouds in the sky. When we remember to separate our attention from our feelings, we show faith in the training and practices we have developed to stay focused.

Start with One Thing

If you don't have a daily practice of quiet and stillness, my question is "Why not!?!" The science is so clear (and there are already so many books on these techniques) that I'm not going to take time here to relitigate each one. I'll just say, for example, that in *Tools of Titans*, my buddy Tim Ferriss found that more than 80 percent of the world-class performers he interviewed had some form of daily meditation, awareness, or mindfulness practice. And my conversations with the most successful, most fulfilled, most creative people in the world reveal exactly the same thing.

If you haven't started down this path yet, don't overthink it. Choose one of these practices—it doesn't matter which one—and give it a few minutes every day. If you already have a dedicated stillness practice, consider deepening it or adding a second one that calls to you. Deciding *where* you place your attention, and then going for it, is an important step toward building a life you can love.

Meditation

Meditation has been proven to reduce stress levels and is correlated with success for many people; however, I believe that meditation on the whole has been misunderstood. Meditation is not static. It's a dynamic process of focusing, mind wandering, then refocusing . . . over and over again. It is simply becoming more aware of how often your mind likes to wander, suspending judgment about this awareness, and then bringing it back to that singular target. The more you do this—whether you train your attention on your breath, a mantra, or a more guided practice— the better you'll become at learning to focus on what's in front of you. "It's like going back home," Dr. Tony Nader, neuroscientist and leader of the Transcendental Meditation (TM) movement, told me. It's like "going back to the source of everything," he said.

Mindfulness

Mindfulness weaves a state of expanded awareness into your entire day so that you can be more conscious of life and less reactive to it. One practice I use is a body scan, where I spend a few minutes every hour or so checking in with the various parts of my body, beginning with my toes and moving up to the top of my head. I also like Kamal Ravikant's idea of taking ten conscious breaths throughout the day whenever he feels anxious or stressed or Wim Hof's breathing exercises, which he recommends doing one to two times per day (you can find examples of this on YouTube).

Prayer

You don't have to be religious to consider prayer as an act of attention. Whether it's the Prayer of Examen, a review of the day's activities before bed, or simply repeating a single word in your mind, appealing to a higher power of our choosing gives us a greater sense of meaning in our lives. Sometimes, when life is truly chaotic, our only resort may be the Serenity Prayer, which is a plea for "serenity to accept the things [you] cannot change, the courage to change the things [you] can, and the wisdom to know the difference." Whatever prayer path you may choose, you are never as alone as you think or absolutely without help or hope.

Journaling

Countless creators attest to the power of journaling as an act of mindfulness and awareness. From creativity experts like Julia Cameron to contemporary comedians such as Mike Birbiglia, many creative people from all disciplines have cited journaling as a tool for clarifying their thinking. One of the most beloved techniques is Cameron's Morning Pages, three pages of stream-of-consciousness, longhand writing *first thing* in the morning. Other people carry a small notebook around with them to document their lives *and their thoughts and ideas* in real time. Whatever works for you, know that when we write things down, we force ourselves to focus on the events in our lives, to reflect and consider their meaning, and to gain some perspective.

Gratitude

We all get distracted from what matters most, but a daily act of gratitude makes it easier to stay focused on what we want to do and why we want to do it. Usually, I write down everything I am most appreciative of at the end of the day, no matter how good or bad it seems. "How we paint the world in our minds," neuroscientist Adam Gazzaley told me, "is guided by our attention and that creates our memories and forms our personality." When we paint our world with things we are grateful for, we rescue the past from regret and create a future worth hoping for.

A Chance to Choose

Learning to direct attention is a lifelong practice.

As you begin to master both internal and external distractions, you will inevitably turn back to the world around you in your quest to direct your attention in ways that bring purpose and meaning to your life. You may know *exactly* where to train your attention, whether you're pursuing a lifelong dream you've ignored, you're tinkering in the garage and teaching yourself to use a new tool, or you're just doing something as simple as reading for pleasure.

But if you have no idea where to begin, there are three ways to get started that will have the most impact—paying attention to your body, paying attention to the people around you, and paying attention to your environment. By using these techniques, you give yourself the best possible chance to have a choice about where and how to focus.

Pay Attention to Your Body

Athletes are some of the best in the world at paying attention. Not only do they visualize success and live in the moment, but they also understand that attention doesn't just originate in the brain. It's a function of the mind-body connection.

According to Dr. Wendy Suzuki, author and professor of neuroscience and psychology at New York University, meditation, sleep, and exercise are all critical for peak attention. Meditation is a no-brainer. The one thing high-performers in every discipline have in common is a meditation or mindfulness practice of some kind. Period. Ditto on sleep. I spent years skating by on four to five hours of sleep per night, but that was dumb. Sleep is the foundation for brain function, and without it, there's no hope for sustained attention. Ignore sleep and sleep hygiene at your own peril.

But what really grabs my attention is what Dr. Suzuki advises about regular exercise, and just so you know, she's talking about thirty to forty-five minutes of daily exercise if you can manage it. "The best time to exercise is right before you need to use your brain in the most important way you need to use it every day," she said on the *Huberman Lab* podcast. That's because for two hours after every exercise session, we get a mood boost and improved prefrontal cortex function, which translates to deeper focus.

We've all felt the mental clarity and rush of endorphins from running, swimming, or lifting, and study after study has proven the connection between a healthy body and a high-functioning mind. Even if you can't exercise every day for half an hour or more, just ten minutes can help you maintain the habit and reap some of the cognitive benefits of more regular, intense workouts.

The other brain-boosting practice Dr. Suzuki recommends is one I've done—at least intermittently—my whole adult life. Cold plunge. Before you skip to the next section, *hear me out*.

Before cold plunge became a trend, I regularly swam in the ocean near our beach house outside of Seattle. Even in the summer, the water never goes much above 55 degrees, and in the winter, it's significantly colder than that. I'm not always excited to get in, but after so many years, I crave the sense of exhilaration and well-being I get afterward, so I do it anyway. Cold plunge has become such an important part of my life that we even installed an outdoor cold-plunge pool at our home in Seattle. You may never go that far—and you don't have to. Just a big blast of cold water at the end of a shower will do the trick. I dare you to try it for a month straight and tell me it doesn't change your life.

Pay Attention to the People Around You

You've heard the saying that you are the average of the five people you spend the most time with. You might have even heard the very meme-able, "Show me your friends, and I'll show you your future." These statements might feel cliché when you're scrolling, but they illustrate an important point: it *really* matters where we focus our energy and specifically who we focus it on.

Choosing who you spend time with is absolutely critical because, as humans, we are insanely adaptable. For better or for worse. If your friends and your work environment are healthy and positive, you will adapt your own mindset, habits, and practices to match. But the opposite is also true, and it's easier than we might like to fall in with people who don't help us be our best selves. This behavior is biological so that we fit in with our tribe since we are a social species.

Though everyone is deserving of kindness, not everyone is deserving of your focus or friendship. That doesn't mean you have to be cruel or insensitive, but it would be wise to occasionally audit your friends and acquaintances. Are these the most uplifting, confident, and positive people you can surround yourself with? Or is it time to seek out people who support your long-term experimentation and growth?

Pay Attention to Your Environment

Have you ever stepped off a plane, emerged into a new environment, and felt absolutely amazing? Or entered a room with exquisite design and feng shui and felt your nervous system relax or come alive in a meaningful way? Or maybe you've experienced the exact opposite. Say you've entered someone else's space and immediately felt uncomfortable or stressed? Think back and try to remember what you noticed in those moments. What visuals, smells, and noises come to mind when you think about a positive or negative environment?

Most of us have *some* control over our environments. We may not be able to control how many people in the world drive electric cars or stop everyone from littering, but we can often influence at least some aspects of the places we work, sleep, and live.

Personally, I find my productivity thrives in places where there is some sense of beauty. Minimalist design and clean spaces free of clutter are key to my ability to minimize distractions. To be sure, what I consider "beautiful" is not what you might like, but that's not the point. The point is we all can do our part to create spaces that inspire us to live and work better.

It's not about having the biggest house with dedicated space for all our activities. Even if it's something as simple as cleaning your desk at the end of your workday or making your bed in the morning, we can cultivate places of solace and greater focus. These little acts of beautifying or bringing order to a space can have an incredible effect on our lives.

Signal versus Noise

A final word about distractions.

They're like Whac-A-Mole, and just when you think you've won the game, they start popping up all over again. In the introduction, I described my own pattern of moving back and forth between playing it safe and playing by my own rules. Attention is a critical factor in understanding those swings and hopefully, eventually, regulating ourselves. Many of us alternate periods of great focus in which our attention is a laser beam with times when our attention appears as a million points of light bouncing all over the place.

But the goal is not perfection. If you decide that nothing else will do, then you will fail.

The goal instead is to bring our attention back over and over again to what matters. We will not always be able to focus as we might like. But the sooner we get better at recognizing when we've gone astray, the sooner we can gently bring ourselves back to the path we want to be on.

As with the description of meditation earlier in the chapter, the plan is not to arrive at a place where your attention does not wander (you can't), but rather to get good at bringing it back to an anchor like breath, mantra, or a spot on the wall. This will be a recurring theme for almost every lever in this book. The aim is not for a perfect state of being for each of these skills but rather to aim for an increasing level of awareness that allows us to come back over and over again to who we are and how we want to be.

Mastering our thoughts and creating the conditions to both rest and do our best work is a never-ending process that takes its own kind of focus. Most people truly *want* to be aware, it's just that we forget as we go about our daily lives. But ironically, attention is a bit like technology . . . unplugging and restarting is the best way to reset. Just do that over and over. Restart again and again. Anyone who is sincere in their endeavors will see results.

Ditch the Shiny Object Syndrome

Years ago, I received an email from a photographer named Abby who was trying to break through in her career. "My challenge," she said, "is that I've got a YouTube channel. I've got a Teachable account. I've got Facebook. I've got *everything*. I've taken out ads. But I'm still struggling to get traction with my creative endeavors."

When I took a quick look at her portfolio, the problem was clear. "I don't know what your 'creative endeavors' are," I told her. "And I don't think you do either."

Most of us, when seeking something we want, tend to neglect the *one* thing we should be doing to get there. Abby was doing too *many* of the "right" things, dividing her attention across too many projects and platforms. It seemed like she was on the right track, but by spreading her attention so thin, she was unable to build a body of work that would have earned her the reputation she so desperately wanted.

To be fair, we can all be guilty of shiny object syndrome. When the novelty wears off and reality sets in, it can be easier to jump to the next thing rather than to face an obstacle or settle into how difficult our current projects might be, especially when we're nervous they won't work or distracted by all the opportunities that are available to us.

Then we're surprised when we struggle to get traction, spinning our wheels and wondering why our efforts amount to less than they might. What's missing for many of us is an understanding of what matters most. "When you know what matters most," writes Gary Keller in *The One Thing*, "everything makes sense. When you don't know what matters most, anything makes sense." As such, this is a vital exercise to any training of attention: Can you identify what matters most in any situation? What if you had to fashion a guess and commit to that? I'd venture a guess that you'd find out quickly that it either was or wasn't valuable.

Quit the Comparison Trap

In 2015, Olympic swimmer Chad le Clos was on a mission to defeat the great Michael Phelps. Le Clos, a South African who had previously beaten Phelps, started a public feud in 2015 when his rival announced that he was coming out of retirement. The reason? Phelps said that none of the swimmers seemed that fast. Le Clos took that personally.

Leading up to the event, both swimmers engaged in a public contest of trash talk. All of this culminated in the 2016 Summer Olympics in Rio de Janeiro, where the world watched as the two Olympians duked it out in the 200-meter butterfly. For the first hundred meters of the relay, they were neck-and-neck. In the second half, Le Clos fell behind. The race ended with Phelps finishing in first place at 1:53.36 and Le Clos placing fourth.

The next day, a photo of Le Clos spread across the internet. It was a picture of Phelps winning his twentieth gold medal while Le Clos swam beside him, a few strokes behind. In the image, the South African is just a head behind the American: mouth open, turned to the side—staring at Michael Phelps. Phelps, however, is looking straight ahead.

Where we place our attention is where we give our power. Awareness of the competition can be a good thing to a degree, but when we put our focus on the accomplishments of others, we leave little energy for ourselves and kill our own momentum. What great performers know is that you are never competing against anyone but yourself. Be different, not better. Sometimes you'll win; sometimes you'll learn. But if you keep growing, you stay in the game.

Boredom Is a Gift

When we become more present, we infuse life with meaning and purpose. The more you pay attention, the more exciting life gets. Contrary to popular opinion, boredom does not come from the object of our attention. Rather, it comes from the quality of our attention. Fritz Perls, one of the psychologists responsible for bringing Gestalt therapy to America, said, "Boredom is lack of attention." Understanding this reality brings profound changes in our lives and helps unlock the magic and mystery of the moment.

According to Manoush Zomorodi, author and host of NPR's *TED Radio Hour*, "boredom is the gateway to mind-wandering, which helps our brains create those new connections that can solve anything from planning dinner to a breakthrough in combating global warming." The key is to sit with the discomfort of boredom rather than running away from it every time it crops up. Zomorodi points to a troubling statistic: in 2007, we shifted our attention at work every three minutes. In 2017, we did it every 45 seconds. Now it's common to task switch every few seconds, all day long, without even noticing. And yet, it's critical to let yourself be bored on occasion, to allow the mind to wander and see where it lands. Who knows what you might find?

I'm certainly not saying you should be perpetually bored. But if you pay close enough attention, if you go deep into something, even something that at first doesn't really interest you, everything you notice should amaze you. This is particularly true if you're used to constantly having your attention stolen by one stimulus after another. Instead of looking for that next fix, it might be good to be still for a while and see where your attention takes you.

Decide Who You Will Let Down

It's not uncommon these days to have hundreds of people who know what you're up to on any given day, simply by virtue of posting about it. But the pressure of "what will people think" can become overwhelming because living a bold life, one you can actually call your own, is scary. A good antidote is to decide, once and for all, who you are willing to let down. (And to remember that no one cares *quite* as much as you think they do because they're all too busy worrying about their own problems.)

This could be as simple as making a short list of people you *don't* want to disappoint. When Brené Brown and I recorded a live podcast in front of an in-studio audience, she showed me a short list of people on a one-inch-by-one-inch scrap of paper that she carries around with her in her wallet. These are the people in her life whose opinions of her actually matter to her—and this stands in contrast to the millions of other people who may or may not have an opinion of her work. People can think what they want, so long as *she* knows that she's accountable to a few individuals who matter most.

A Tiny Experiment

I wish I could tell you that attention is limitless. But it's not.

There's not a single person on this planet who couldn't get better at paying attention. Not the Dalai Lama. Not Roshi Joan Halifax, Tara Brach, Jack Kornfield, or any other spiritual guide. And certainly not any one of us neophytes.

My wife, Kate, actually studied with Tara and Jack for two years, and both were very deliberate in encouraging their students to practice the power of awareness and attention. Kate has a quote from Jack scribbled in one of her journals: "One form of delusion is lack of attention. We live in a culture of chronic inattention fed by the frenzied pace of modern life. When we are lost in thought, half asleep, we don't notice what is happening. It is like the experience of driving to a destination, parking, and realizing that we have no memory of the whole drive. Mindfulness training wakes us up from this trance to see more clearly, to experience the aliveness of our days."

Whether you've been training your attention for years or you're just getting started, I encourage you to try a tiny experiment. Set your alarm for four to six random times during the day, and when it sounds, take notice of where your attention is. Is it on the present? Your awareness of what you're doing at that moment? Or are you thinking of something else? Take a beat and bring all of your attention back to the present moment.

Again, the goal is not to "get it right," but rather to simply become aware of your own attention. Then and only then do we have a starting point and a greater sense of the challenges we face in staying present or reckoning with the next lever: time.

Lever 2

Time

The Magic of Presence

There's a magical thing that happens in life-and-death situations that makes it very clear that time is malleable. Whether you've experienced this or not, you're probably familiar with the idea that, whether during death-defying stunts, car crashes, childbirth, or flow states, time slows way down. Milliseconds can feel like minutes. This is not to say that you should seek life-and-death situations, crash your car on the regular, or increase the size of your family by a factor of 10 just to alter your experience of time—you probably don't want most of the downstream effects from these events—but rather to remind you that time shifting is a normal phenomenon.

Though the goal of this thought experiment is just an intellectual understanding at first, the further you go down the rabbit hole, the more you see that time is *very* elastic—and not just at the edges of our daily experience. It is *always* expanding and contracting, dilating and constricting, ebbing and flowing.

I'd bet your experiences—when closely examined—will back this up.

Consider everything from a boring job—or even a boring set of tasks in a job you love—that makes time feel as if it's trickling by too slowly to time flying when you're reading a book or, even more significantly, watching your kids grow up. Then ask yourself: What is my day-to-day relationship with time? Do my days stretch out before me endlessly or do I have enough time to do all the things in life that I want to do? Do I constantly wish for "more" time? Am I worried that all this hurrying and scurrying about leaves me feeling rudderless and adrift? The answers may surprise and alarm you, but . . .

The good news is that I've seen the promised land.

Time management is dead. Flow states and time dilation are real—and this is just the tip of the spear. We can and will use this lever to experience both the delicious sense of presence we discover in the now and the fullness of our lives, which stretch out before us.

And no, it's never too . . . ahem . . . *late* to begin.

Take Brent Underwood. As a longtime digital media manager and hostel owner in Austin, Texas, he spent his days working with renowned authors and digital superstars while his nights and weekends were reserved for an active friend group he enjoyed. In spite of all that, when a friend he respected and admired asked him, "So what's your thing?" he realized he didn't have an answer.

On paper, he was a success, but when Brent quieted his mind and paid attention, he knew something was missing. He liked his work, he liked his friends, but he also longed for a purpose bigger than himself. To make matters even more complicated, he was deeply conditioned—as so many of us are—on one particular point. Specifically, he couldn't help but be afraid that taking a leap of faith and trying to live a bigger life would come at the expense of the pretty good life he was already living.

Fast-forward just a month to when everything changed.

With a tiny ding, a magical text message arrived from a friend. Right there in the palm of his hand was an article: "Buy Your Own Town for Under a Million Dollars." Though it might have seemed foolhardy to some, in just a few days Brent found himself standing in the middle of an abandoned, hardscrabble town that had broken its fair share of ambitious men and women before him. But, for some reason that was unclear at the time, he was not deterred. He loved history, he loved hospitality, and he knew *he* could build a community around the ambitious dream of rebuilding this bygone place.

He brought on investors, took out a loan, and used every penny he had to become the owner of Cerro Gordo, a ghost town perched high above Death Valley. Once the site of the largest silver mine in California, the men (it was quite literally all men) who once worked there had pulled more than $500 million in ore from deep within the mountains. That money, together with water from nearby Owens Lake, allowed for the explosive growth of Los Angeles in the 1950s and '60s and drained the resources of the little town that made it all possible.

Now it all belonged to Brent.

A couple of years into ownership and he's already gotten everything he wished for and a whole lot that he wouldn't have wished on his worst enemy. Fires, floods, earthquakes, and perhaps strangest of all, fame.

In June 2020, he moved to Cerro Gordo full time and shortly after that the centerpiece of the property, the historic American Hotel, burned to the ground. Since then, he's lost thirty pounds and lives in a desolate place with no running water that is far from modern conveniences. Every day, he says, is "chaos with a side of adventure."

And yet, he's found his dream.

He's in love with his new life in a way he's eager to explain to anyone who will listen because he's living out the mission and purpose that always eluded him before.

When we spoke in February 2024, he appeared on my screen from nine hundred feet underground, deep in a mining shaft complete with a makeshift recording studio where he gives interviews with media, works on his wildly successful YouTube channel "Ghost Town Living," and takes solace in the winter from the subfreezing temperatures up on the surface.

With help from volunteers and supporters from all over the country, he's rebuilt the hotel during the past three years—the roof had gone on just before our conversation—and he has created an elaborate master plan for a carefully crafted resort, complete with museums, stargazing, and more.

He knows that to many his decision to buy Cerro Gordo might have seemed reckless. His decision to live there full time, mostly on his own, even more so. But in the wake of the hardships and the reconstruction, Underwood stumbled on perhaps the most valuable and beautiful aspect of his journey: his own understanding of a new relationship with time.

"I used to get a lot of anxiety thinking, 'What's next? What's next? What's next?' I think a lot of creative people are like that," he said to me when we spoke last. His refrain sounds like a lot of ours—either seekers who haven't found their passion despite getting on in years, or high achievers who are on a soulless treadmill of one achievement after another, seeking meaning and purpose that they just can't find. But Brent's life completely changed when he discovered this little mining town in the Sierra. "I used to always worry about the future, or dwell on the past. But now I've found presence, and this presence has given me purpose. I know that I have time. I know what the next project is. I've found a huge amount of comfort just knowing that Cerro Gordo is all this and more. I'm hopefully going to be focusing on this till the day I die."

At the intersection of working with his hands, building community, and telling stories about this magical place sits his next adventure, one that allows Underwood to finally put the brakes on hustling. No more being busy for the sake of looking or feeling important. By focusing on Cerro Gordo, he can give the power of his full attention and, just as important, his time to rebuilding the town. Projects that start out seeming impossible—like delivering high-speed internet to the depths of the mine—may take months of planning but have come together through ingenuity and determination. And what was once a monkey mind spent chasing the next big thing now is a calm and quiet experience of presence and dedication to reviving Cerro Gordo.

"As soon as I got to Cerro Gordo," he says, "there was suddenly time for everything, even though I knew this project would take decades."

So much of what came before in Brent's life was about

weighing options, deciding what to do next, and figuring out if his life was "going the right way"—which is really just a sloppy euphemism for the way that most people have been conditioned to live. Once Brent stopped playing it safe, living the life expected by others, and settled on a new path—as different as it might be from what you or I would choose—his life and his relationship with time were entirely transformed.

Before Cerro Gordo, Brent filled his days running, but now that he's focused his attention on one mission that comes from deep inside him, time has thrown its door wide open before him.

This is but one example of how the world's most interesting and remarkable people are leveraging time. No longer is time a steady state ticking in the background of an eroding life. The new lens on time—and what Brent and others like him know—is that we can shape our experience of time simply by being deliberate about what we do and how we do it.

Up until now, you may have packed your schedule full of work and events, cramming as much in as you can and moving from one activity to the next without ever slowing down. But let me stop you there. There's nothing noble or romantic about being busy. It just means you don't have your shit together. This is not to say that hard work and long hours might not be required to get you to where you want to go. Whether you leave it all behind and move to a ghost town or somewhere else far, far away is up to you. But *all of us* can live with a more expansive sense of time right now regardless of our circumstances simply by making some important choices and taking some specific actions in our lives.

FACT: People who are awesome at life are not obsessed

with their calendars. They know that time is malleable. Often, they glide through life, aware of what needs doing and doing it, all the while shifting from one experience to another, leaving open space, and living in the present. For these people, there are always enough hours in the day to do what needs to be done because they've let go of everything but the work, play, relationships, and other aspects of life they care most about. They understand either intuitively or through hard-won experience that "managing time" never works. Instead, they've learned to surf it, to catch, dial in, and ride waves of time according to their own intentions. Sound too good to be true? Stick with me.

In the previous chapter, we talked about training your attention on the things that matter most, and in this one, we're going to talk about time as its counterpart. It's a delicate balance between a practical approach with the realities of clock-time schedules and systems, and an entirely new consciousness that will change the way you see time and your place with it.

Life Is Long

I grew up hearing that life was short and we ought to make the most of it. You probably did too. Our friends, teachers, and parents meant well. They put that phrase on repeat to get us to make decisions and act. While I'm all for action over procrastination and overthinking, the toxic, unspoken message that underpins "life is short" is that there just isn't room for mistakes, turning inward, or true creation, so—enter a familiar phrase—you'd better play it safe. Be sure to get it right. Moreover, you'd better decide on your path [insert career, relationship, schooling here] quickly, or else you'll waste your life away.

But I find myself thinking, "what if flailing around without purpose and being terrified of making a misstep is an equally awful problem? What if rushing and desperately trying to hit benchmark after benchmark is very clearly a recipe for disaster?" Unfortunately, that's both how and why most people live in fear, play it safe, and end up navigating according to a prefab plan without really considering if the life they're building is the one they actually want.

It's specifically by allowing outside pressures and the artificial, rigid plans of others to shape our days that we get off track. High school. College. Office job after graduation. Make sure not to miss a beat. A few short-term relationships. Serious relationship, marriage, kids, buying a house. Check. Check. Check. Check. Check. All of a sudden, we wake up to find we've been living life on autopilot. Instead of discovering life, uncovering each chapter as it naturally unfolds, and living for our own creativity, joy, and fulfillment, we're chasing someone else's idea of the good life. In the words of David Byrne: *This is not my beautiful house, this is not my beautiful wife!*

I've been there several times myself. When I made the decision not to go to med school and later on when I left grad school just short of my PhD in philosophy of art, it wasn't easy. I was embarrassed to admit I had embarked on an uncertain path as a photographer and was frightened every minute about my future. But one thing kept me going in those early days.

When I finally started being deliberate about how I spent my time, my world expanded.

Statistically speaking, most of us reading this book are time billionaires, which investor Graham Duncan defined as someone who has at least a billion seconds (or thirty-one years!) left to live. What this means to me is that time is both precious *and* an abundant resource. But you wouldn't know it in a culture that screams that you must decide what you want to do with your life at twenty-one and get going immediately.

Before any of the haters chime in, "I can't believe you're suggesting we live anything but a passionate, urgent life!" just stop. Let me explain that there is another way.

Depending on how you count, I'm on my third or fourth career and at least my third life arc (also count dependent)—and I plan to have a few more during my next billion seconds. What I've learned through my own ups and downs is that there are invaluable lessons in screwing up and screwing around. In fact, there is no "wrong" path. Whether you believe it or not, you can cultivate freedom and take the time to try new things, take risks, retrace your steps, reinvent yourself, and discover again and again what will cause you to come alive. It's only once you stop trying so hard to accomplish something every minute that you'll see that no experience is ever truly wasted.

I like to think of following our curiosity and attention as "purposeful drifting." As long as we're listening to our intuition and remaining aware, we're free to have all kinds of experiences: some good, some bad, some even boring and anticlimactic. We are not androids—we learn through experience—and therefore, we must do new things in hopes of stumbling upon how we are meant to live out our days. We may, in fact, sometimes be many people, trying on different costumes and roles, each helping us understand and refine who we are and what our story is about. This journey is what allows you to see what you are truly made of and where you were meant to go.

Lucille Ball, the comedian, didn't get her big break until she was forty with the launch of *I Love Lucy*.

Momofuku Ando, the Taiwanese inventor, created instant noodles in 1958, two years before his fiftieth birthday.

The underground poet and musician Leonard Cohen toured the world for five years straight when he was in his seventies, playing sold-out stadiums and recording three new albums, the last of which was released weeks before his death.

Carmen Herrera had her first retrospective at the Whitney Museum of American Art in New York City at one hundred years old. The list goes on and on.

That's not to say that you ought to wait around to make your mark but rather that our timelines are ridiculously flawed. To the outside world it probably seemed that life had passed these geniuses by, that they were "wasting" time pursuing their dreams. But it's not up to other people to define how you spend your time, whether you reach some sort of milestone in your twenties or your eighties. It's up to you to short-circuit over-thinking and outside pressures, however small or large, and take action in the direction of your interests. After all, life does require that you participate in life, so what if you were methodical with how and where you spend your energy? What if you used what you learn as valuable data about who you are, what you're good at, and what you love? And then went after it time and again, and again, and again.

What your career counselor, your parents, and your peers have you worried about is that this venture takes so much *time*. In response I'd say, yeah, but what is a life if it's not the experience and process of living your dreams and finding out what you love from a place of purpose and presence?

The best life, the most creative life, is unfolding one perfectly imperfect scene at a time. We can agree it would be silly to get up in the middle of a riveting movie, walk out of the theater, and say you didn't like the ending. This is what's magical about where you find yourself right now with this book in your hand, or as you listen to me read it to you: You're right in the middle of the plot—who knows where this thing is headed? It's precisely your job as the artist of your life to *live it out and find out*. As Francis Ford Coppola once said, "It's so silly in life not to pursue the highest possible thing you can imagine, even if you run the risk of losing it all. You can't be an artist and be safe."

The Now Is All That Exists

The past is gone, and the future isn't here yet. All we ever really have is *this moment*.

"Be here now," as the spiritual teacher Ram Dass liked to say to his students seeking enlightenment. I can sense a little eye roll right now. You've heard this a million times? Okay. Let's be real—most of us aren't that worried about enlightenment. We just want to put down our phones, be present, and focus on the joy or the work in front of us. We can't wait for tomorrow or next month or next year to get started. We have to begin being in the now *now*.

But what the hell does that really mean?

The great wisdom traditions are correct in telling us that the present moment is all there is. The past is over—we can't go back and change it. We can learn from it and not make the same mistakes again, but it's gone. On the flip side, the future is an illusion. Quite literally we will never arrive *there*. We set goals, we can imagine our future selves, but we can only act in the present in service of those goals. And it is precisely the process of dwelling in either the future or the past that leads to suffering. As Eckhart Tolle puts it in *The Power of Now*, "The more you are focused on time—past and future—the more you miss the Now, the most precious thing there is."

Instead try to imagine life as an infinite paper chain of "nows" strung together. No loop is any bigger or more important than another, no matter what our thinking mind may tell us. We have experienced thousands of nows before this one, and we will experience thousands after this one, but all we have is the now that is happening in the one moment in which we are existing this very second.

This is why life-or-death situations are the ultimate illustration of how the power of presence has the capacity to change time. One of the scariest but clearest experiences in my own life was when I got caught in an avalanche during a back-country photo shoot. I felt the snow pile down the mountain, gradually engulfing me and sending me down the hill with it. At that moment, probably for no longer than ten or fifteen seconds, time stood still. As I tumbled under the snow at forty miles an hour in complete darkness, my experience was one of absolute presence and pure consciousness. I was able to run through a very detailed protocol—a series of increasingly intentional and dramatic efforts designed to help me escape my predicament. It wasn't until the fifth or sixth item on my what-to-do-to-save-my-life list that I somehow managed to navigate my tumbling, racing body out of harm's way.

I was absolutely tuned in to the moment. And in hindsight, those few seconds gave me enough time to observe, analyze, react, and experiment until I found a solution. Even now when I think about the avalanche, I remember the sensations, the absolute calm, and the distance I felt from my own fear. There was zero judgment about my predicament, only a clear sense that there was a challenge before me that I was required to overcome.

I was truly in the now. We always are; we just don't remember. I've tried to stay there ever since.

But I don't.

In fact, I'm not really very good at it, just like you may not be.

I'll be at dinner worrying about my book deadline, I get distracted by a random thought during a podcast, or my mind drifts during meditation. This is real. This is life. *No one* manages perfect presence 100 percent of the time. *But* I also don't let myself off the hook. The moment I realize I'm dwelling in the past or projecting into the future, I stop. I don't feel bad; it's a practice, so I just guide myself back to what I'm doing. Because the *now* is all that exists.

Play an Infinite Game

Knowing that life is long and living into each and every now are both critical, but alone they aren't enough to reset our ideas on time and rethink how we make the most of the months, years, and decades in front of us. We have to go further and consider, really consider, if we want to play by the rules society has established or if we want to make our own rules regardless of the consequences.

The world is full of people who want to keep the current systems in place and who will take your decision not to play it safe as a personal threat. If you opt out, if you make different choices, they no longer have the same kind of leverage over you that they once might have. You've reclaimed that leverage for yourself.

Life can be a creative process, a game where we are continually remaking the rules. This doesn't mean there aren't challenges and privileges to consider or that chaos and luck aren't factors, but what we ultimately end up with is something we have either created or settled for. Though you've probably heard someone described as "winning at life," there is no winning—not really—especially if you decide you're playing an "infinite game."

The late New York University professor James Carse distinguished between what he called "finite games" and "infinite games." A finite game has a clear finish line with winners and losers; in an infinite game, the point is to keep playing forever.

Chess, for example, is a finite game. Two players come to the table and play the game according to an agreed-upon set of rules. There's a clear winner and loser, and when the game is over, that's it.

Hula-hooping is an infinite game because the goal is literally to keep the hoop spinning no matter what. Whether it sits on your hips the whole time or you move it to your leg, your arm, or neck (if you're really good!) doesn't matter. Nor does your success or failure have anything to do with anyone else. You just keep doing your thing, and with any luck, you and the other hula hoopers cheer each other on and inspire each other with new ideas and ways of playing the game.

The biggest problems arise when we apply a finite game mentality to an infinite game like life. If you're playing it safe and following someone else's map, life can feel like a mad dash to the end, one in which you're constantly comparing your progress to other people's and trying to collect as many accomplishments as possible. I can't say for sure that everyone who lives this way ends up unhappy, but I've met a few people who can't celebrate their own successes, let alone anyone else's.

But if we treat life as an infinite game, then everything takes on a more interesting shape and scale. With fewer or no mandated milestones out ahead of us, you no longer have to be concerned with "doing it right" or falling on your face. You can focus on your own curiosity and then create a future that only you can imagine. In an infinite game, as long as you're moving forward, learning, and growing, you're doing great. Even failures become valuable lessons. The real tragedy, then, is not failing at what we attempt but measuring the whole thing with someone else's ruler.

So how *do* you measure a life? We use metrics that extend beyond the realm of degrees, money, and fame and that take into account the ups and downs of being alive. If life is long, we're living in the now, and we're playing an infinite game, there is room in this one precious life of yours to fail and try again, to grow and shrink, to reinvent yourself more than once. There is space for all kinds of beautiful things—if you are willing to not just find the meaning of life, but to create it.

Go with the Flow

We all know the beauty of flow when it happens. We're ten times more productive than we usually are with what feels like minimal effort. Our sense of time disappears, and we feel that perfect level of engagement and relaxation, which signals the release of dopamine and norepinephrine into our brains and the reduction of cognitive load, which allows us to focus on what's right in front of us. Many people assume it's a mythical state that we can't call into being. It turns out that's all wrong.

Cofounder and executive director of the Flow Research Collective, Steven Kotler has spent years researching and writing about this topic, and one piece of data always stands out to me when we talk: we don't have to wait for flow. Neuroscientists have already discovered twenty-two flow triggers or strategies we can reliably use to get into flow in our lives *every day*.

Ironically, the one that seems most obvious and attainable to me is complete concentration, which gets me and so many others closer to the sense of timelessness we all associate with flow. You can't control a dog barking in the distance or someone unexpectedly coming to the door, but you can address the biggest concentration killer by silencing your phone, putting it in a drawer out of reach and out of sight, and turning off all notifications on your computer. We all know we should do this, but few of us reliably do.

The second time-based strategy I regularly use (and have been using for years even before understanding why it worked) is carving my work into 90- to 120-minute blocks throughout the day. If I want to address a problem or go into a special creative headspace, that's the minimum amount of time I need to make progress, and it's the one that most reliably creates conditions for me to experience one or a combination of other flow triggers such as autonomy, novelty, complexity, and creativity.

Sometimes I put my head down and just work on one thing. Other times I fill the block with a bunch of batched tactical stuff that needs to get done, such as meetings, phone calls, and tasks that tend to take away time from big projects. Whether I dedicate these blocks to solving a single big problem or to tackling smaller to-dos, I can organize my entire day around them. And during each ninety-minute period, I work my ass off and stay militantly focused.

I find tremendous freedom when I'm focused and free from distraction for long periods of time. And working like this helps me get more done by working less. You can't add hours to the day, but you can have more energy, vigor, and focus when you allot a certain amount of time to get the work done (more on the power of constraints later). For me and so many others, these ninety-minute periods are the fundamental building blocks to my day. Sometimes I'll put two blocks together in a big strategic chunk, so instead of being hyperfocused on a project for ninety minutes, it's three hours. After some practice, I was surprised by how much more effective this made me.

I freakishly protect the first ninety-minute block of my day for my morning routine. It's the one thing I know can make a huge difference in the success of my day, week, and life. Sometimes this requires modifications, but I generally go way beyond reason to keep this block intact. What I do during this time may vary, but it always involves some level of self-care, exercise, and some form of mindfulness to get mentally focused for the day.

After that, I prioritize the next ninety-minute block as the most important stuff I need to get done that day. By knocking out the essentials early, it's easier to keep going knowing you've made great progress. Then, the rest of the day is just whatever needs to get done that's already scheduled.

These two strategies are my preferred method to set myself up for flow. Discovering the flow triggers that work for you will take some experimenting and a willingness to find a new way of working and living, one that may be different from what you're doing now or even different from what most of the people you know do. But that's part of the deal because a steady rhythm is essential to making sure you have the time you need to do what matters to you.

Choose Flow

Flow is a magical place, but you don't have to wait for inspiration or a fairy godmother to take you there. You can get into flow every day once you identify the trigger that unlocks flow *for you.* It may be curiosity, novelty, or shared risk or some combination of the twenty-two triggers below. Kotler and his team at the Flow Research Collective have divided these triggers into four categories, and they look like this:

Internal Triggers

Cognitive Factors That Spontaneously Lead to a State of Flow

- Autonomy—you're on your own by design
- Complete concentration—you're focused on one thing only
- Passion, purpose, and curiosity—you're in alignment with your values
- Immediate feedback—you know where you stand and can course correct in each moment
- Clear goals—you have certainty about your objective
- Challenge—your skills are required for the task at hand

External Triggers

Techniques That Induce Flow during a Specific Task or Activity

- Novelty—this is dynamic and new
- Risk—there are consequences at play
- Complexity—multiple variables require a certain level of focus
- Unpredictability—the outcome is in part determined by your actions
- Deep embodiment—a completely immersive experience

Creative Flow Triggers

Strategies That Aid in the Creative Process

- Creativity—cultivating a new and original idea
- Pattern recognition—connecting the dots that others might miss

Group Flow Triggers

Factors That Promote a Collective State of Flow

- Shared goals—shared objectives create belonging and commitment
- Close listening—actively connecting breeds trust and understanding
- Yes, and—the cornerstone of improvisation and contribution
- Sense of control—empowerment and belief
- Blending egos—team dynamic and mutual respect
- Equal participation—inclusivity and talent recognizing talent
- Familiarity—honoring what's unique in everyone
- Constant communication—the free flow of ideas
- Shared risk—we're all in this together, and that matters

(Source: Flow Research Collective and Steven Kotler)

Time for Rest and Renewal

Traditional productivity literature suggests that we should rest *because* it will make us more productive. While that may be a nice by-product, the reason to rest is really because we were designed to rest. We must sleep to live, rest to recover. For us humans, taking some sort of regular breaks is a feature, not a bug in our code. It's required.

Without blank space, we can't have new ideas let alone come close to achieving flow or anything else. The key is to practice "strategic renewal," an idea that Tony Schwartz, founder and CEO of The Energy Project introduced to me once over a hot cup of coffee.

Strategic renewal is a simple strategy that I cannot live without, and thanks to Tony, I regularly employ. After every ninety-minute block of intense focus, I carve out thirty minutes to rejuvenate myself physically and mentally. Most of the time, I get up. Walk around. Eat a snack or have lunch. I go outside and smell the fresh air. I call my wife and check in with her, see how her day is going. Basically I create empty space and let my mind float free or I do something fun (more on that later) that gives my brain a rest.

Sometimes, I use my lunch breaks as either an "eating meeting" or "walking meeting" (sometimes both), but generally it's time to get some headspace before the next work chunk. These intentional pieces of time—working and not working—mean that I can keep my attention on what matters when it matters, increasing my chances to find flow on command.

The idea is that we may not be able to increase the hours in our day, but we can certainly increase the energy and determine the focus in our hours, allowing us to live well and more peacefully in the time we have. Taking scheduled breaks throughout the day rejuvenates and restores you both physically and mentally, helps you stay in the now, and allows you to move through those necessary to-do's as a meaningful aspect of life, rather than as the chores you've been taught to believe they are.

Beyond building in smaller, daily breaks to our workdays, we also have to consciously take longer periods of rest and renewal. These big chunks of "away to play" time can exist within our regular schedules in the form of a morning, afternoon, or full day of golfing, bike rides, hikes, family time, or whatever helps you relax and take a brain vacation. There's also filmmaker Tiffany's Shlain's tech shabbat or executive leadership coach Wayne Muller's *Sabbath*, both of which suggest that a day of rest can be a sacred act regardless of your relationship with God or religion.

Finally, there's always taking an actual vacation, too. And when I say "take a vacation," I mean turning on an "out of office" message and checking out of regular life. The most common refrain I hear is that it's not possible, that your world or your company or your life will fall apart without you.

If this sounds like you, pause for a moment to examine that belief. For most of us, it's simply not true. That's not to say that carving out time away isn't difficult or sometimes fleeting at best, but it pays to remember this important idea: it's important to choose your rest days or your body will ultimately choose them for you in the form of sickness and disease. Without rest, we're done for.

Get into the Now

Life-or-death experiences have a way of concentrating our attention on the now, but what about the rest of the time? What about when we're doing the dishes? How can we realistically exist in the present without turning into adrenaline junkies? Here are a few ideas.

Systems over Schedules

We all have meetings, doctor's appointments, and restaurant reservations. We have to get shit done on a schedule, but if you can create a life that feels both novel and entertaining within some of the basic (and even necessary) parameters, then the weeks and years will feel long in retrospect.

My solution is *systems over schedules*. What's the difference? Schedules tend to be rigid and are often dictated by others— they're the timetable that the world imposes to keep everyone moving in the same direction in the same way. Systems, on the other hand, are the practices and routines we establish to support ourselves and keep our creativity and adaptability in shape in a world that has other ideas for us.

When I first started creating systems around what I needed to do to become a thriving, professional photographer, the outcomes I'd been longing for started accelerating, and I had more time to spend on the activities I loved.

Now I no longer have to look at the calendar and negotiate with it to see what I can accomplish within the handful of spare minutes I have on any given day. Instead, I shape my time around what matters most to me, like movement, meditation, and walking to get coffee with my wife every morning *no matter what*. Those routines set me up to do my best work and give me a sense of direction and agency over my life. And somehow, even though a regular morning routine technically "takes" time from my day, the clarity and creativity that bubble up from these daily practices end up "giving" me time to fit in everything I truly want to do.

You Can't Do Everything

We've already talked about reclaiming your attention from distractions, but the corollary when it comes to time is that you must actively *decide* what you're going to do and, more importantly, *what you're NOT going to do*. To get into the now, we have to own our time. Claim it. Stake it out. And then we have to stop doing the stupid stuff that only makes us *look* busy and productive.

"You wouldn't even really want to be able to do everything, since if you didn't have to decide what to miss out on, your choices couldn't truly mean anything," writes Oliver Burkeman in *Four Thousand Weeks*. "In this state of mind, you can embrace the fact that you're forgoing certain pleasures, or neglecting certain obligations, because whatever you've decided to do instead—earn money to support your family, write your novel, bathe the toddler, pause on a hiking trail to watch a pale winter sun sink below the horizon at dusk—is how you've chosen to spend a portion of time that you never had any right to expect."

As a culture, we must stop celebrating "busyness," aka unfocused activity that results from and contributes to the anxiety so many feel. World-class athlete, actor, and politician Arnold Schwarzenegger couldn't help but comment in an interview about the fact that everyone is worried about finding time to do what they need to do. But that's not how it works, he believes. "You don't find time. You make time." Cliché as it may seem, it's true. Time, and how we experience it, is something we shape to our own ends.

Stretch Out Your Timeline

One of my wisest friends on the topic of time (read: recovered from "time management and now actively shifts time in his favor"), Tim Ferriss, suggests that one way to get into the now is to deliberately create opportunities for time dilation. In one example, he describes a weeklong hiking trip in the mountains of New Mexico where the combination of a new location, a novel topography, and an environment of constant change dramatically expanded his sense of time. "Thinking back to the morning of day two or day one felt like looking back to three weeks or four weeks prior."

In his estimation, we can deliberately use this strategy to design our lives to take advantage of experiencing time in this way. If each year we schedule two, week-long trips and each of those trips—by intentionally engineering them to be filled with novel and dynamic experiences—gives us a feeling that weeks or months have passed then we are effectively extending our *experiential lifespan* (what it feels like to us) by up to fifty percent, or six months! That's a non-trivial extension of life based almost entirely by choosing carefully what we do and how we do it.

The End of Waiting

Even when we know that presence is the ultimate gift we can give to ourselves and others, we often can't help but look to the future while ignoring the present—"killing time" while waiting for a moment that may never arrive.

But why would we kill time when *now* is all we have?

Enjoy it. Be here for it.

In *The Power of Now*, Eckhart Tolle talks about giving up waiting as a state of mind. Waiting devalues the present moment, encouraging time to "pass" without giving it the benefit of attention. As such, I'd encourage you to run a tiny experiment.

The next time you're "waiting" in line for coffee or "waiting" in the doctor's office, replace *waiting* with *practicing being here*. Avoid making a call, scrolling on your phone, or planning a trip to the grocery store. Just be right where you are. Feel your feet on the floor. Notice your breathing. These moments are not intermissions from your life. These moments are your life. Rather than giving it away, choose instead to be here for the remarkable, stunning, and beautiful experience of being alive.

Lever 3

Intuition

The Art of Trusting Yourself

"Mayday, mayday, mayday. This is 1539, we hit birds. We've lost thrust on both engines . . ." radioed the pilot to air traffic control. About ninety seconds later, at 3:31 p.m., the plane hit the icy waters of the Hudson River.

In the realm of human experience, there are moments when split-second decisions can mean the difference between life and death. Such was the case on January 15, 2009, when Captain Chesley "Sully" Sullenberger, faced an unimaginable crisis at 2,818 feet above New York City just seconds after taking off from LaGuardia Airport. Everything about the flight was routine—until it wasn't.

After a collision with a flock of geese created a sudden and catastrophic loss of engine power, the Airbus A320 started to plummet toward the densely populated city below. While his copilot worked the checklist for engine restart, Sully took control of the plane. Standard protocol—and air traffic control from the tower at LaGuardia—dictated that the pilot return to the airport or divert to nearby Teterboro Airport in New Jersey, but Sullenberger's intuition told him that these options were not viable. "We can't do it," he said. "We're gonna be in the Hudson."

Being a pilot means an endless series of checklists and procedures with no deviation or improvisation. It's a profession that trains the intuition right out of you. But in spite of all that, Sully knew in his gut that attempting to reach an airport was not an option. It would have been a recipe for disaster that would have killed everyone on board plus any number of people on the ground. In that critical moment, the plane descending with its engines eerily silent, Sully made the decision to do what had never been done before in commercial aviation: to attempt to land the airliner, belly down, on the surface of the Hudson.

As the aircraft rapidly lost altitude, the captain relied on the instincts he had honed over decades of flying to guide the stricken aircraft toward the frigid waters below. As a former fighter pilot from the 1970s and '80s with more than 19,663 flight-hours, including 4,765 hours in the A320 that he was piloting during this incident, Sully had more than forty years of experience in the air. But unlike most other commercial airline pilots, he was also a certified glider pilot who knew how to fly *and land* an unpowered aircraft. With remarkable composure and clarity, he executed a textbook-perfect emergency water landing, bringing the plane down with minimal impact and ensuring the safety of all 155 people on board. Today his feat of bravery is referred to as the *Miracle on the Hudson*.

As investigations into the incident unfolded, including rigorous scientific modeling and analysis, it became clear that Sullenberger's reliance on intuition had been the key factor in the successful outcome of the emergency. Even the National Transportation Safety Board ultimately affirmed that ditching the airplane provided the highest probability of passenger survival, given the timing and circumstances. And while standard protocol had certainly provided a foundation for his decision-making, it was Sullenberger's intuitive understanding of the situation, informed by decades of experience and expertise, that ultimately saved the lives of everyone on board. His intuition and willingness to defy convention not only averted disaster but illuminated something that all of us feel, but which we're conditioned to ignore: the feelings in our gut.

It was those same gut feelings that told neuroscientist Jill Bolte Taylor exactly what to do when she suffered a severe hemorrhagic stroke in the left hemisphere of her brain. As someone who had researched strokes in other people for decades, she found herself calm and collected as her own experience unfolded in real time. A highly trained neuroanatomist, she was in a unique position to observe her body and brain when the stroke began and she felt the brain functions responsible for language, analytical thinking, and linear processing beginning to shut down.

In her TED Talk and subsequent book, *My Stroke of Insight*, Taylor described making a clear, seemingly intentional transition into a heightened sense of intuition and spiritual awareness in that moment, and she credits her intuition during the once-in-a-lifetime event as a unique vehicle to better understand the experience of a stroke. After she recovered, Taylor reported a sense of surrender to the stroke in order to perceive it more clearly—time dilated, and she was able to pay closer attention. Even as it was happening, she saw it as an opportunity, trusting that giving into the unknown rather than resisting the moment would provide her with the best insight and would allow her to transcend the rational approach to understanding the mechanism and experience of a stroke.

The presence of mind to fully experience this moment, and specifically to listen to her intuition around it, provided Taylor a unique opportunity for scientific discovery, but she also credits it with being especially valuable in accessing a special guidance that was helpful throughout her recovery.

Once you start to pay attention, it's obvious the important role intuition plays in so many stories of survival . . . and daily life. Few others have taken the volume and quality of risks that Travis Rice has and lived to tell about it. Universally hailed as one of the world's all-time greatest big mountain riders, Travis is almost always the guy in the most epic segments of every snowboard film from the past fifteen years. When asked about his ability to stay healthy, alive, and "safe" (in quotes here because he makes a living engaging in extremely dangerous activities) under these conditions, he attributes his continued presence on earth to luck, but most of it to various kinds of very specific training.

Unsurprisingly, Travis trains in the craft of snowboarding year-round and has for most of his life. There's physical fitness, mindset training, nutrition, route finding, and a hundred other subskills in which he is among the most elite *ever* in his field. But he told me over a beer that he's found just as much power and wisdom in leveraging his intuition as he has in all of his training. Of note is his reliance on what he calls his first reaction—his "gut" reaction. He always trusts and acts on that initial reaction regardless of his own resistance or any impulse to talk himself *out* of it. It is a critical distinction that he's quick to call out as something that differentiates him from other elite athletes.

Rice credits legendary guide and snow safety expert John Buffery for helping him manage these factors on the bleeding edge of the sport: "One of the beautiful rules that has come into existence for how we operate in the backcountry is that the minute you make a decision to step back from something—say for example the crew is going out in the backcountry and something doesn't feel right, and you hesitate or step back . . . you see something in the snow pack or in a [avalanche assessment] pit—that's the step for the day, that's it . . . you don't talk yourself out of that. When you are heading out for something risky, you feel yourself make a change in your momentum or inertia that is a hesitation and you pull it back . . . we don't second guess it."

Whether we're responsible for hundreds of lives or simply protecting our own, these stories illustrate one important truth: the feelings we have all the time—each day around small and large moments alike—are not to be ignored. If you're not used to tuning in to what you really want, it might not be obvious where to begin, but I'm here to tell you that intuition is not something you need to create from scratch. There's a quiet place inside that's already available if you're willing to be still and listen. Where Sully, Bolte Taylor, and Rice differ from most people is that instead of relying on conditioning or external sources of wisdom, they turn to their own inner voice, recognize its value, and faithfully lean into what it has to say.

Now it's your turn to do the same.

We've all had experiences in which we've felt a powerful force within us guiding us in the direction we're meant to go. Whether we've heeded that message is another story, but if we want to stop playing it safe and start finding our way in the world, intuition is key. So let's begin to leverage this exceptional tool residing within you.

Seeing What You've Been Taught to Ignore

In the realm of decision-making, conventional wisdom once held up the conscious, rational mind as the pinnacle of reliability and efficacy. We believed it to be thorough and deliberate, the bastion of sound judgment. However, the latest insights from psychology challenge this notion, revealing that the conscious mind, though deliberate, is often slow and prone to fumbling. It's as if we're navigating on foot through an elaborate labyrinth with just a headlamp—we can't get around very fast, and we're only able to illuminate a small fraction of the complete path at any one time.

What we now know is that intuition is a far more powerful yet enigmatic process operating beneath the surface of our conscious awareness. Drawing upon past experiences, internal signals, and environmental cues, intuition guides us toward decisions with astonishing speed, often bypassing the conscious mind entirely. It's as if a gentle whisper and an electrical shock had a baby—intuition can in a millisecond urge us in a direction we may not consciously comprehend but that we somehow feel or "know" to be right.

The latest neuroscience is well aware of the complexities of intuition. Our brains process vast amounts of data—so much so that millions or perhaps billions of data points per second, an estimated 90 percent, needs to be filtered *out* of our conscious mind so as to avoid cognitive overload. This fact combined with other evidence suggests that our bodies, perhaps our gut cells, and some subset of the 36 trillion other cells that make up a human, serve as reservoirs of accumulated wisdom, storing insights gleaned from past experiences.

Under certain conditions, some scientists postulate we gain access to this reservoir, tapping into a wealth of information that lies beyond the realm of conscious thought. Yet, despite its profound influence, intuition remains one of the most elusive and enigmatic aspects of the human experience. It's a capacity that exists within us all, and yet our understanding of it is still quite limited, like a muscle whose strength we've not yet fully developed.

If you find yourself hesitating and doubting your ability to trust your intuition, know that you're not alone. It is perhaps the most powerful tool in our body's arsenal but also the one we know the least about. Unfortunately, society has conditioned us to prioritize the rational over the intuitive, to mistrust the whispers of our inner knowing, and it has come at a huge cost.

Few tools in life are more of an antidote to playing it safe than one's intuition. So rest assured, the capacity to trust yourself lies within you. Whatever forces are at play—whether metaphysics, the quantum field, placebo, or space monkeys, it doesn't matter—those who refuse to play it safe don't need to understand the specifics of these mechanisms. They know through the emerging science, stories like those in this book, and their own experience that only a fool would ignore such power.

Trust Your Gut

The world will sell you a map to guide your life journey with a little red dot that says, "You are here." In theory, if you follow the tidy line of dashes over the river, through the woods, and across the valley, you'll get to your destination. Or at least to the destination where you're supposed to go. All you have to do is go to a certain college and get a specific set of grades, then you'll get the "right" job, and all will be well. But what if none of that makes you truly happy? What if you're not fulfilled when you get to the destination? Or even more likely: What if that map is complete trash and following the dotted line actually lands you no closer to the desired destination than flipping a coin?

It's time to forget the map and look to your internal compass to show you the way. The difference between the map and the compass seems small at first, but it's significant. A compass points only in a general direction. It is clear in its pointing, but it doesn't pretend to care what is between you and your destination; it simply trusts that you will navigate the details. A map, however, shows a specific route. At first it seems to be more useful because it tells us exactly where to turn right or left, but its precision actually sets us up for struggle. In the dynamic nature that is a human life, it's a lie that there is only a single path that will lead us to our destination. This is why the compass—aka your intuition—is the preferred tool for navigating life. It knows that small detours are a part of the process, but no matter what, our true north matters most.

We all have a dream or an idea or a longing that we were taught to park or ignore or parse out because it's impractical or embarrassing or somehow just not "what we're meant to be doing." I'm willing to bet that something immediately came to mind when you just read that sentence. But if it didn't, close your eyes and think about your past experiences. *What lit you up? What have you loved?* You don't have to have a fully formed idea. You might just have the vaguest idea of your dream, and that's good enough. Just look at that thing for a moment, whatever it is, and acknowledge it. You don't have to *do* anything at first. You just have to stop pretending that it isn't there. Your internal compass will tell you where to go next.

When you're ready, expand this. Start experimenting, start spending time, actual minutes in your day exploring your idea, walking in the direction where you want to go. As soon as you begin, you'll feel an energetic pull that's not been there before. I have talked about the massive uplift that comes from genuinely paying more attention, and this energy is a 10x version of that. Remember, this isn't about upending your entire life. Rather, by simply increasing your awareness of your dreams, dedicating time to them, and moving toward them in ways that make sense, you will experience a real sense of progress. The goal then becomes to repeat this process.

But beware: you can't think your way into this. You absolutely have to take action. I say that now because this is the part when most people freeze. Even if your compass is clearly pointing you in a certain direction, we *all* have some sort of "magnetic field" that can make the needle spin around or point the wrong way for a beat or two. *You want to make it as a musician? I wouldn't do that. It's risky.* Then, all of a sudden, the needle gets wobbly and starts to lead you away from your true north. Plenty of times, misdirection comes from the people you love most telling you to play it safe. They're trying in a very loving, caring way to help you, but their approach is all wrong.

Playing it safe is actually the riskiest thing you can do.

Following someone else's plan or fulfilling the dreams someone else has for you will never make you truly happy. The number one concern of the dying is that they've lived the life that other people wanted rather than the one that they chose for themselves. So consider yourself lucky. You are aware of this pitfall *right now* and have the capacity—the duty even—to defeat it in its tracks and set alarm bells in place for any time it crops up in the future.

The world is changing faster than it ever has before. Imagine all the tech jobs that didn't exist ten years ago. The variations on what a "family" looks like. Or how much the idea of "work" has changed just in the last decade. Such changes are an opportunity, a chance to exercise your intuition in service of considering how you live and work best. It's not easy to get started, but *audentes Fortuna luvat* or fortune favors the bold, a precept which is particularly true when it comes to navigating away from the illusion of safety towards a more meaningful, creative life based on your intuition and the other six levers in this book.

You will make mistakes, head in the wrong direction even.

But no effort is ever wasted. And no move is too small. If you're reading this book, maybe the yearning you feel for something more is new, or maybe you've been asking yourself for a while, "Is this all there is?" Whichever it is, in the next sections, we're going to figure out how to find stillness, to reconnect your brain to your gut, to unearth the physical signs of intuition, and then to move in a direction that allows you to live more authentically even if there's a short-term cost.

An Intuition Field Trip

Your intuition wants to be heard but can easily be drowned out by so many factors present in this modern world we live in: technology, anxiety, busyness, multitasking, hurrying, and disconnection from the body, to name a few. To reconnect with your intuition, you must slow down and create enough space to hear the whisper of your own internal knowing.

Give yourself a Saturday—reminiscent of Julia Cameron's "Artist Date" from her legendary masterwork *The Artist's Way*—and fill the day with whatever you are drawn to do. First, set aside your technology. And then, since intuition lives in the body, start your day with a walk outside in nature (a park if you are urban) and really tune in to the sensations in your body. What do you feel, smell, and notice? Let your awareness expand to find a calm joy in this state of connection and relaxation as you walk for as long as you desire.

When you're ready—and throughout the day—let your guiding question be: What next? Listen to the soft, small voice of intuition for guidance. Feeling hungry? What sounds delicious? Listen. Go pick up some groceries or consider a few favorite restaurants. Practice keeping your attention in the body, in the moment. Feelings of expansion and openness in the body signal "yes—follow this!" and any feelings of constriction or contraction suggest you should choose differently.

What next? Feeling tired? Take a nap. Seeking adventure? Go on a hike, head to a flea market, or explore a museum. Dance at home, sit in a park, or paint. Whatever tugs at your desires and lights you up in the moment, do that! And stay off of your phone. Feeling stuck and don't know where to start? What did you enjoy as a kid? What do you often wish you had time to do? Let yourself be right about a few things in the same day. No busyness, no hurry. Simply listen, act, and notice.

At the end of your experiment, reflect on the process. How were you able to listen? What did you feel? And for extra credit if you can muster it: Expand this exercise to begin the night before. Hop in bed without any technology. Don't set an alarm. Fall asleep naturally. Wake up when you are rested and begin your day of intuitive listening and doing. Be sure to include a moment to rejoice in reconnecting with the part of you that truly *knows* what you want at the deepest level and then bring this practice with you into all aspects of your life to continue to exercise this muscle and develop your intuition.

When Success Isn't Enough

Amanda Crew had everything she ever thought she wanted.

From the time she was little, she dreamed of becoming an

actress, and when, at ten years old, she was cast in the musical *Dragon Tales*, her dream began to come true. Life sped up, and she started filming commercials and training at the prestigious American Academy of Dramatic Arts in New York before booking a few small roles in television and movies. By the time she was thirty, Amanda was a full-fledged part of the Hollywood machine, running to auditions to acting lessons to the gym and back again. Now that everyone knew her from HBO's *Silicon Valley* and from movies like *Sex Drive* and *She's the Man*, she couldn't slow down or else she risked losing it all.

"Then, everything collapsed in on me," she told me as she described the dark night of the soul that descended right around her thirtieth birthday.

"From the outside, my life looked great. I was still working on *Silicon*. I had a beautiful partnership with my now-husband. But inside, I was miserable, and nothing made sense anymore. All these things that used to make me feel good and empowered and worthy and valuable—suddenly, all of it felt meaningless."

Despite her "grasping to try to make it work," she couldn't stop crying. *I have everything my childhood self wanted*, she thought to herself. And yet, somehow, it just wasn't enough. She had to hit the brakes and stop running for the first time in almost twenty years. And when she did, she could finally hear her intuition telling her that the life she was living wasn't going to work anymore.

Amanda still loved acting, but the stillness she created for herself is what made it possible to see that the pace she was working at wasn't working, despite the long-standing pattern of making hay while the sun is shining in Hollywood. For it was precisely that pattern that was crushing her soul and tricking her into trading her health for another paycheck or another role. To her credit, she did something unheard-of in that business: she took a break—a definitive, multiyear break—during which she started experimenting with projects that interested her. She tried photography, tackling a one-hundred-day project in which she captured and shared images every day, and she also worked in an after-school program for girls. But most of all she stopped, consulted her internal compass, and began to meet her own needs for the first time in a long time.

When we talked last, Amanda told me that she's started taking more time off between projects as a chance to reconnect with her intuition. "You know," she said, "orange trees are not always creating oranges. There's a winter where they shed everything and everything has to die and fall off to then nourish the soil and the tree; to then regrow a whole new thing. . . . To be constantly producing is just too much."

Sometimes our intuition will tell us to act, and sometimes it will signal us to pause and give ourselves a break, not necessarily at the most convenient moments. But when we get off the hamster wheel and create some stillness for ourselves, we're able to see the way forward much more clearly. Intuition is much harder to access for many people during the heat of battle.

Following your intuition doesn't have to be dramatic, for it's as natural as breathing. It's not necessarily quitting your job, leaving your family, moving to Mexico, and taking up painting. Rather, it's a quiet knowing that can help you decide what to do or not to do. It's a function that you are born with, and just like a muscle, it gets stronger and healthier the more you use it. Choose it or lose it.

The Body-Brain Connection

The world around us may be rapidly changing, but one thing that isn't changing nearly as fast is the human body. That's why one of the first steps in rediscovering your intuition is to reconnect your head and your gut.

When you first start to pay attention, your intuition may be quiet, especially if you've spent years suppressing it or you've been conditioned (as many of us have) to defer what you want to some future moment. If you can't hear your intuition right away, never fear. That's where your gut comes in.

We've all had the experience of being so nervous we want to throw up, so excited we feel butterflies, so depressed we don't want to eat, so anxious that we spend all day running to the toilet. No matter how your feelings manifest in your body (and each of us is different), they show up whether we ignore them or not.

Next time you have to make a decision, notice how your abdomen feels. Are you clenching your abdominal muscles or are you standing up tall and relaxed? Is your stomach gurgling or achy or do you feel at ease? Can you eat or do you feel that you're forcing yourself to take just a few bites? Whether you want to acknowledge them or not, all of these are signals about your well-being. If you're having a hard time zeroing in on "what's next?" or "what you really want" and your intuition is quieter than you might like, it's sometimes easier to take action and then do a gut check. I guarantee the answer is there.

We are deeply conditioned to push through, to ignore the signals our brains and our bodies are sending us. But doing so exacts a cost. For a while, we may be able to ignore our intuition, but at some point, the truth of who we are and what we want will demand attention. Maybe persistent stomach problems, maybe burnout, maybe something else, but it will be obvious that we can't keep going the way we've been going. Hopefully you don't need to get to that point, but it's never too late. Your intuition is always there for you, one of the most important levers for a creative life.

How Do I Know It's My Intuition Speaking?

If you're early in the game, new to making decisions based on intuition, you might second-guess yourself, and it can be hard at first to keep going. This is because you're not getting the kind of external validation you may be used to getting. Here is a non-exhaustive-but-hopefully-helpful list of internal signals that your intuition is at work:

- **Body signals**—Pay attention to the physiological responses, such as a "gut feeling" or a sense of calm, that may indicate intuition at work. (This is why attention is critical.) During the years I've been practicing body awareness, I've honed my skills to be able to quickly sense what is "true for me," which presents as a gut feeling of expansion and possibility, even joy or optimism, in my body. It's a levity, a "wow, what if?" feeling. The opposite of this is a constriction, or a biological sense of closing down, which often comes in the form of a desire to "think something through" and a shift to intellect and reason.

- **Immediate impressions**—Notice your spontaneous thoughts or feelings and contrast them with the slower, analytical process of conscious reasoning. For me, Derek Sivers's "It's a hell yes, or it's a no" decision making framework always comes to mind and is easily leveraged when I'm tuned in and seeking a sense of where I stand on a topic. At its core, this approach encourages me to only lean in or commit to the things that truly resonate with me, rather than spreading myself too thin by accepting lukewarm or mediocre opportunities. I use this for everything from attending dinner parties to accepting speaking gigs to deciding what creative project to tackle next.

- **Past experiences**—Reflect on moments in which your intuition proved accurate, usually in a snap judgment or moment-based experience sort of way. What were the outcomes? This is a classic "I knew I should have listened to my instincts" sense of regret that we've all had, not dissimilar to Travis Rice's rule of shifting momentum—namely, that when you feel or vocalize a shift in your feelings based on a combination of past experience and current/immediate response, you do not go back on this decision.

- **Energy alignment**—Look for sparks of energy or little bursts of confidence . . . a genuine feeling that you are on track. That's your intuition at work. If you keep going, more of this activity could in turn produce more energy. In my body, this feels like an eagerness

for more or an awareness that says, "I love this!"
Energy alignment is one of my strongest signals, and I
never ignore it.

- **Emotional alignment**—Intuitive feelings often
  align with positive or negative emotions. Genuine
  intuition tends to evoke a sense of rightness or
  wrongness about a situation. People who are super
  feelers, neuroatypical, or highly sensitive often report
  a distinctive awareness of virtue alignment (i.e. this
  is good/true or bad/false) and are rightly reluctant
  to enter a logic-based review of how to make a
  decision downstream from feeling these emotions.
  In my more limited experience with this form of
  alignment, I've come to believe that most people
  either disproportionately feel the energetic variety or
  the emotional variety.

- **Quiet mindfulness**—Practices like mindfulness
  and meditation can help quiet the conscious mind,
  allowing intuitive insights to surface more easily.
  As a practitioner of Transcendental Meditation aka
  TM, I often make use of the quiet, calm moments
  immediately following morning or evening meditations
  as a window where I can ask my heart to reveal itself
  on items in limbo or on decisions I need to make.

- **Athletic Mind**—A phrase used by renowned sports
  psychologist Bob Rotella, athetic mind describes the

moment when someone clearly envisions an outcome and then trusts the subconscious to deliver as opposed to tediously and consciously reviewing every aspect of a skill. Skills are critical, of course, and mastery helps, but whether you're shooting a basketball or hitting a golf ball, if you're thinking about anything but a steady picture of the target, then you're doomed to perform sub-optimally. When athletes—or by extension anyone "trying" to do a thing rather than just doing it—are obsessed with details (e.g. fundamental aspects of technique and sequencing), it makes successful outcomes virtually impossible. In other words, Yoda had it right: "Do or do not. There is no try." The simple goal here is to drive technical repetition to the point of mastery and then focus the mind entirely on the target as a form of trust.

With all of the above, when you start to pay attention, your intuition will show up in one or often several of these ways at once. The more you pay attention, the more you will see and eventually trust these experiences as reliable guides.

Beyond Right and Wrong

A week before Glennon Doyle went on the road to promote her book *Carry On, Warrior*, she learned that her husband had been unfaithful to her throughout their marriage. The couple decided to work on the relationship, attempting to reconcile, and Glennon began writing her second book—a marriage redemption memoir that Oprah Winfrey had already selected for her famous book club.

However, from the time she had learned of her husband's infidelity to the release of her second book, Glennon came to realize that she had a secret, and it was eating her alive. Glennon was in love with another woman. At this critical point, she could either bury her truth and tour the country talking about reconciling with a man she was now planning on leaving—or she could come clean.

This wasn't an easy call. There was a lot of pressure to make a big splash with the book. And coming out, in more ways than one, would expose Glennon in a way that was scary and that would have familial, financial, and professional repercussions. But keeping it all in wouldn't feel great either.

Close friends advised her to wait six weeks before making the announcement. If she went on tour with news of a divorce, the book would likely fail. Who wants to read a redemption story about a marriage that's ending? One agent told Glennon that if she told the truth, it would be career suicide.

For over a decade, she'd been an advocate of LGBTQIA+ rights, creating a net of inclusivity with her audience for those who didn't necessarily fit into societal norms. But she'd also been a prominent leader in the Christian community, serving as Sunday school teacher, mother, and Christian author who regularly spoke at churches. No matter what she did—spoke up or stayed silent—she would be out of step with at least one group whose support she had relied on.

Of course, she wanted to do the *right* thing, but which

"right"? There was the "right" Christian response she'd learned in church. And then there was the "right" approach her fellow feminists recommended. At this point, Glennon had been sober for thirteen years, and her sobriety had been based on one thing: integrity. Yes, there would be consequences for telling the truth, but playing it safe was no longer an option.

Glennon knew that she needed to honor her inner wisdom, regardless of the cost. She'd asked friends and peers and mentors, but now she needed to ask *herself*. Quieting down the external noise, she tuned in to her own inner wisdom to figure out what *that voice* was saying.

Deciding she'd rather commit career suicide than "soul suicide," Glennon broke the news publicly. Turning her own world upside down, she left her husband for a woman and told the world about it. Since then, her bravery has inspired millions of other people to listen to their intuition, and Doyle has gone on to write more bestsellers and build an even bigger fan base of followers, friends, and supporters. Most importantly, she's built a family and a loving relationship with her wife, Abby Wambach.

Of course, there's a cost to leaving behind the pack and going your own way. It's probably no surprise that Glennon's community—the same group of people she'd offered a safety net to for years—rallied around her in the time of her greatest need. Just as we learned from Brent Underwood's story, to get something great, we often have to give up something good. In Glennon's words, the challenge with a situation that is "good enough" is that it can tempt you to settle for less than you deserve.

Ultimately, settling for "good enough" undermines your long-term authenticity because as soon as you aim for "great" and do something unexpected, the whole house of cards comes toppling down. And even if that doesn't happen, the best possible outcome is you succeed at someone else's game—which is not what you want to do. To paraphrase the late Stephen R. Covey, you end up climbing a ladder in life only to realize it's leaning against the wrong wall. So you might as well choose what's right for you as soon as you know what it is and forget trying to play by other people's rules.

The Wake-up Call

The hardest part about building a life is understanding who you really are underneath all the layers of performance and achievement. Most people never get there, but if you dig deep, what you find just might surprise you.

With a law degree from Cornell and a partner-track job at a prestigious law firm, Rich Roll was miserable in a successful career. At thirty-one, he admitted he had a drug and alcohol problem and spent the next nine years getting sober and rebuilding his life.

"I went from this guy who's gonna be a senator," he told me, "to . . . dirtbag status. . . . When you medicate throughout your entire adolescence and twenties, you're creating a barrier between you and your consciousness the entire time. When you finally remove that . . . you don't know who you are; it's very confusing and disorienting."

During those early years of sobriety, Rich was still attached to his old definition of success, which was largely derived from impressing others. What drove him was the desire for his parents and friends to see him as a respectable person. "But that was all bullshit," he realized. Unraveling his old identity was a process that took Rich years. Over time, he began to understand himself as something separate from a list of impressive accomplishments.

One night just before turning forty, Rich felt a sharp pain in his chest while walking upstairs. For someone who had been an athlete his whole life, this was a big deal. At the time, he wasn't obese, but because he had spent the majority of his thirties bringing order back to his life, he was working a lot and eating fast food to keep up with a busy schedule. Fifty pounds overweight, easily tired, and feeling like his life was lacking purpose, Rich knew more change was needed.

"It was a symbolic moment," he remembered, "in which I realized that [even though I was sober,] the way I was living my life was just untenable. . . . It was another bottom. For me, it was similar to the day I decided to get sober. I had this palpable sense that once again I was having one of those moments that . . . could be a catalyst for another major lifestyle change."

Not long after this second wake-up call, Rich paused and tuned in to the newest guidance from his intuition. Although he had already made dramatic changes, he switched to an all-plant diet and started running and doing endurance workouts, culminating in a 320-mile Ultraman race consisting of swimming, biking, and running. After this first race, he continued to compete, including completing five Ironman-distance triathlons on the five islands in Hawaii—in less than a week. The lesson here is obviously not about vegan diets or a week of five triathlons. It's about getting wise to the warning signs that show up in our lives and realizing that we owe it to ourselves to create the change we say we want.

Since then, Rich has written multiple bestselling books and continues to host one of the most popular health and wellness podcasts on the planet. But just a few years before this, he had no idea who he was and what his life was about. He listened deeply to his authentic self and created meaning in his life.

The Benefits of Compounding Trust

Once upon a time, if you looked in any reference book or did any kind of internet search for "person who doesn't trust their intuition," you'd likely have seen my picture. That is, until I met my wife, Kate.

We first crossed paths on a beach just after high school, she with a group of her girlfriends and me with a pack of buddies. You've heard all those stories about "love at first sight," and yet, while that was not my experience with Kate—even though I noticed her and felt an immediate connection—something *was* different than what I feel when meeting most other people. Sparks were present at that initial rendezvous, but no fire. As luck would have it, our families were living in the same city at the time, so we reconnected on a short date when we were both home during our freshman year of college. I'd gone out with plenty of other girls and been involved in other long-term relationships, but she had a special quality I couldn't quite place.

That's the thing about intuition. It's like rediscovering the joy of childhood games—blindfolded but trusting, spinning in circles until you find yourself exactly where you're meant to be. Or hearing a song and sitting up, immediately transfixed by the sound. I still remember the first time I heard *Smells Like Teen Spirit* during college on the way to a game. The way it electrified my body and drilled into my soul had nothing to do with whether or not it was "cool." It opened a portal to an inner world I didn't know well yet, and I felt on some level that this music had been made for *me*.

Of course, that sense of "knowing" was even deeper when it came to Kate. She stuck with me in a way I still can't explain, from our incredible first date through the four years we fell out of contact while attending schools 1,500 miles apart. Somehow we both trusted that this was for the better. It didn't occur to me that she was "the one" nor did I see then that her perspective—and trusting *the very experience of reveling in her difference*—would change my life.

When we met again, I finally recognized that these feelings transcended traditional attraction by every measure and couldn't be ignored. All along it had been my intuition that had kept me on notice. Kate may have been introverted, shy, and quiet—so different from my typical girlfriends—but she had a radical power that I couldn't resist.

We started dating long-distance when I was a senior in college, and then we traveled in Europe together for six months after I graduated. Being with her helped me understand that the emotional payoff I received from dating a certain kind of person I was used to wasn't worth it. If I had listened to other people's ideas about who would have been a good match, I would have missed out on the biggest win of my life—being with Kate—and that would have been the tragedy of a lifetime.

If you can stick with me here for just another moment, this story is about a more profound insight than simply how meaningful it can be to be in love and married to an extraordinary person. It's this: the universe paid me back for taking this chance. Ever since I truly trusted my intuition about Kate—that she was the special "one"—my intuition began to snowball in ways that I never could have imagined. For example, it was Kate who helped me realize that the payoff I might get from the world for going to medical school (or doing a million other things that seemed prestigious or successful but that weren't really for me) wasn't worth sacrificing my dreams.

Increasingly, each instance of trusting my gut built on the previous one, and before I knew what was happening, I'd remembered how to listen to my intuition. To say this transformed my life would be a radical understatement. I would never have quit grad school. I would never have become a photographer. I would never have done any of the things that eventually brought me to the understanding that safety is an illusion we've been conditioned to accept. Never before would I have imagined that a *love* story would turn into a *life* story about the compounding power of trust.

I tell you all this not just because I enjoy revisiting the story of how I met my wife, but also to emphasize that when your intuition comes knocking—whether it's about a person, a project, a trip, or something else—*listen up*. Being with Kate for the past thirty-one years has been a massive unlock and a goldmine of health and happiness. And I believe that she would say, because she read this and told me so (lol), that the same is true for her.

I've never looked back, largely because as soon as you start to listen to that voice and get good at trusting yourself and what it tells you, amazing things can happen at a radically compounding rate. This is what people who stop playing it safe learn really quickly. Once you start looking for the leverage your intuition offers, you end up seeing it everywhere—you can't *un*see it—and it becomes the master catapult and a foundation for a deeply meaningful, fulfilling life.

Lever 4

Constraints

Constrain to Retrain

"I'm stuck," I said.

"How? What are you working on?" Austrian-born Stefan Sagmeister, one of the world's heavyweight champions of graphic design and a foremost creative thinker, asked me.

"I need to generate cover design ideas for my book. It's about creativity," I said several years ago as I was working on *Creative Calling*. My wide eyes, the bounce of my eyebrows, the head tilt, and the worried expression on my face signaled to Stefan that I perceived this as an enormous, slightly terrifying creative challenge. I was particularly worried about designing a book package that lived up to the book's promise I had articulated so clearly on the back cover—that reading it and living by its principles would give you vast creative superpowers! The meta nature of the task was something that Stefan immediately grokked, and he launched into teaching me one of the most valuable techniques for creative ideation I've ever known, one that I still use to this day.

Developed by legendary, lateral-thinking expert Edward de Bono, this powerful creative ideation process involves thinking about the solution to your problem from the point of view of something that has nothing to do with the problem you're trying to solve. In the case of my book design, for example, Sagmeister held up a full glass of drinking water and explained how thinking of the book through the lens of all the attributes of this glass of water could yield an entirely new and innovative set of design ideas.

What if the book cover were clear?

What about reflections? Could that be a part of the design?

What if there were some conceptual tie between the "flow" of water and the state of creative flow that so many artists seek?

All of a sudden, by implementing a very basic constraint on the ideation process, it was as if a dam broke inside me. The ideas—solutions to my problem instantly began to flow . . . like water. And within thirty seconds, it was also obvious that wherever we landed with this design experiment, no one would ever be able to guess where we'd started. But they'd know for sure that they were holding a book that was unique.

When we finished brainstorming, Sagmeister explained just *how* this ideation process works. The brain is a pattern-recognizing machine, so when we ask it for solutions to problems, it generates answers based on what we've *done* before. *What worked last time? Let's do it that way again.* The synapses in our brains have been wired together through repetition, so like water flowing along the easiest path, the brain's natural instinct is to fall into the familiar grooves in our neural wiring.

But if we reject the initial, most familiar idea because it's not a good enough answer to our challenge, then the next thing our brain generates is a possibility based on what we've *seen* before. The brain quickly rummages through all the recent, sticky experiences it's had and delivers some copycats or something only incrementally different (in the case of my book, a change in color, font, or size, for example) as the next set of possible solutions to the inquiry.

Unsurprisingly, this is the point at which most of us typically capitulate and choose an obvious and immediate solution, which ends up being similar to all the other ideas out in the world already. But copying is a beginner's game. We're aiming for originality.

Sagmeister suggests, via the work of de Bono, that we can *only* land on something truly innovative when we force ourselves to frame the challenge differently, by filtering it through a completely unrelated object or idea. In the case of my book's design, the goal was to reinvent the "book-y" package by introducing new and different constraints that didn't necessarily have anything to do with books at all. That's the strategy that ended up working for my book and the strategy I think works best when it comes to building a creative life.

No matter who we are or where we come from, life will

inevitably impose constraints on us. That's why the idea of self-imposed constraints is a brilliant—and perhaps even *the most powerful*—point of leverage on the path to overcoming almost any challenge. As stoic philosophers have suggested for more than two thousand years in response to such a process (and the title of pal Ryan Holiday's 2014 book): *The obstacle is the way.*

For what it's worth, it was ultimately de Bono's technique, which I used half a dozen times with different constraints, that led to the final book package design, which probably contributed, in some way, to it becoming a bestseller.

Using constraints to generate new ideas may feel counter-intuitive at first—and antithetical to our culture's focus on more, more, more—but only by setting limits can we view potential opportunities, connections, and solutions through a new lens. Even though it may not feel like it, constraints give us a much-needed framework for exploration. It's as if the very act of limiting the breadth creates space for depth, which yields the most interesting results.

Consider the constraints we employ when building a house. The first, and one of the most critical, is the location of a particular lot. We cannot even begin to build without ruling out a million other locations. Then we must assess the land itself—the size of the lot, the soil conditions, the grading, whether or not it's in a flood zone, and the codes that govern exactly what can be built. Then it's time to decide on the number of bedrooms, the materials, the paint colors, the font on the welcome mat, and so on and so forth.

You see where we're going here—building a house is nothing *but* constraints, one after the other. That's the case with so many things we build, whether it's a business, a family, or a life. When everything is possible, nothing is possible. But when we lean into external and internal constraints by choice, the possibilities, ironically, open up to us.

The science around constraints is clear. In cognitive psychology, for example, studies have shown that constraints enhance creativity by focusing our attention-based resources on a wider array of possible solutions and more innovative thinking. The field of neuroscience similarly demonstrates that brain activity is more precise and focused when constraints such as sensory input regulation and task specificity are in place, which leads to more efficient and effective decision-making. And behavioral economics has shown that when resources typically used in solving particular problems are more scarce, it yields increased focus and more creative solutions to those problems.

And yet most discussion of constraints focuses on external rather than internal constraints. Of course, any kind of constraints can be useful under the circumstances, but if we want to use constraints as a lever to build a creative life and play by our own rules, then it's up to us to tap into what we've got to produce the best results for any particular situation. Here are four types of constraints you can enlist to help you solve interesting problems with surprising results: *self-imposed*, *externally-imposed*, *perceived*, and *environmental*.

Self-Imposed Constraints

Self-imposed constraints are simply the limitation frameworks we intentionally place on any problem set in an effort to drive focus to a more elegant solution. They usually come in the form of:

- **Numerical constraints.** These are data-oriented constraints specifically devised to hone focus. Some examples include timeboxing (place a seemingly tight timeline for deliverables on any task), scoping (deliverables will be measured on size, weight, volume of any kind, as in a scaling of the deliverable to better fit a timeline), frameworks, and budgets. For example, to finish my novel by January 1, I will write 500 words per day, preferably between 9 and 10 a.m. when I'm least likely to get distracted.

- **Creative constraints.** These are similar to scoping constraints outlined above, but they are specifically found in pursuits where data is less useful. Examples might be limiting color, style, or genre in photography, painting, or drawing. For example, I will paint an abstract (rather than representative) still life only using blues and purples.

- **Human constraints.** This is an example of overtly choosing with whom you're willing to spend time and with whom you are not. Some people energize you, others drain you, so choose wisely. For example, one of my biggest red flags is indecisive collaborators. If a creative collaborator can't commit to making decisions after lots of discussion or several meetings and revisions, then it's a sign that person won't be a good match . . . namely because they lack the ability to trust their own intuition. Essentially this boils down to an alignment of values on some spectrum that you alone determine.

When we deconstruct the lives of many of the world's most extraordinary people, we can see the role that self-imposed constraints have played in their creative success.

Writer Roxane Gay has adapted a whole body of written work to the social platform X (formerly Twitter), where she regularly shares her perspectives on race, gender, and culture in small but powerful bursts. The constraint of character limits doesn't inhibit her; instead it's become a tool for her impactful commentary, showcasing her ability to distill complex ideas into brilliant, concise, hilarious, and sometimes cutting insights on anything and everything. For Gay, constraints aren't limits; they are the canvas for her powerful posts, which allow her to engage with a wide audience and foster discussions on important social issues.

Or take Chris Ballew, the lovingly quirky founder of the platinum-selling nineties rock band the Presidents of the United States of America. Chris understands what limitations can make *possible*. "That's why I play two- and three-string guitars," he told me.

Early in his musical career, Chris was constantly breaking guitar strings. When the cost and time to replace the busted strings got to be too much, he began experimenting with purposely removing half the strings on his guitar and using heavier-than-normal strings for the others. Before long, he had pioneered a new sound and style. Mika Salmi, the A&R executive that signed the Presidents to Columbia Records, said of Chris, "It was such a cool, simple, and unique sound, that I was immediately drawn in. . . . I remember in the music video for [the song] 'Lump,' you can see that Chris has just two strings on his guitar." Ballew's preferred instrument at the time became a *basitar*, a two-string bass with reportedly 0.060 gauge (C#) and 0.036 gauge (G#) strings.

The Presidents' lead guitarist, Dave Dederer, also played his *guitbass* with a three-string setup, one .065 gauge (C# low), one .045 gauge (G#), and one .035 gauge (C# high) string. This configuration produces a chord whenever all the strings are held down on the same fret, regardless of the fret. That's something he never would have discovered if he had stuck to the standard method for stringing the guitar.

Chris recounted to me with delight the power of these really simple constraints. "It forced me to figure out new ways to make the chord," he said, knowing that it was, in part, these creative limitations that contributed to their unique sound as a band and caught Salmi's ear, all which collectively factored into going on to sell more than three million records.

Externally Imposed Constraints

Externally-imposed constraints arise from events, actions, or outcomes that are completely out of our control. It's useful to think of these constraints as facts that are empirical: both real and demonstrable. Examples of these types of constraints would be the following:

- **The weather.** Let's face it, we can't control the weather. It simply "is what it is."

- **A human condition.** A person doesn't choose a cancer diagnosis or sickness. There are innumerable developmental constraints that may have downstream effects on what's possible.

- **An event.** It's not a stretch to understand that car accidents and flat tires happen, people win the lottery, and we've all lost our keys.

If we analyze the lives of those who experience these types of constraints and yet continue to show up as happy, successful, and fulfilled, we typically see a clear pattern of resilience and a specific, intentional drive to "flip the script" on circumstances beyond their control.

The artist Frida Kahlo knew this better than most. The victim of a traumatic bus accident when she was only fifteen, she was literally impaled on a metal bar, and was forced to learn the hard way how to make art from limitations. With her spinal cord significantly damaged by this accident, she never fully recovered, spending her life in and out of hospitals. On top of that, she had a chaotic marriage to another prominent artist, Diego Rivera, and had to fight for respect as a portrait painter in the early twentieth century, during a time and in a field where women's contributions were not highly valued.

These struggles followed her throughout her short life, but instead of using them as an excuse to play it safe and *not* create, she decided to play by her own rules and used her circumstances—her constraints—as fuel. "At the end of the day, we can endure much more than we think we can," she said, echoing the experience of Frankl, Csikszentmihalyi, and Zamperini. That's not to undermine the real hardships that she or they were forced to encounter. But it does hold all of us to a much higher standard whereby we actively look for a way to see constraints as a path to a desired outcome.

Oksana Masters is a seventeen-time Paralympic medalist and the most decorated American winter Olympic or Paralympic athlete ever. She has graced the cover of *Sports Illustrated*, the *New York Times*, and the *Players' Tribune*, and has one of the most compelling stories in sports.

Born in 1989 in Khmelnytskyi, Ukraine, she is a survivor of in utero radiation poisoning from the Chernobyl nuclear disaster in 1986. For her entire life, Oksana has had to manage severe physical impairments, including having only one kidney, webbed fingers, six toes on each foot, a partial stomach, no right bicep, and no thumbs. Her left leg was six inches shorter than her right, and both were missing their respective tibial bones. Abandoned by her parents, who were unable to accept the reality of her condition, Oksana lived her early childhood in Ukraine's state-run orphanage system. She moved three times before being adopted by an American mother at the age of seven.

Though her move to the United States was life-changing, her hardships were far from over. Within the course of the next seven years, Oksana experienced a series of health challenges and surgeries, including a double leg amputation. Yet in the face of these difficult circumstances, she was determined to make something of her life. Thanks in part to the extraordinary support from her mother, who was a college professor, she excelled in academics. And as her confidence in her own physical abilities grew, she began following her intuition and pursuing her love of sports at age thirteen. Over the next several years, her participation and skill in a variety of sports skyrocketed, and by 2010 she was competing on the world stage in rowing, with other sports like skiing, biathlon, and cycling soon to follow. By the time she was a young adult, she was making history.

When I asked Oksana about her experiences, she was very clear that "nothing is decided before you try." Because she had no choice but to embrace her physical constraints, she applied herself in ways—with sport in particular—that she might have otherwise not. And by taking on seemingly impossible tasks with sports, she learned more about herself than she might ever have otherwise, adding new psychological, emotional, and physical resources to her toolkit that she could apply to other areas of her life.

As traumatic as it was, Oksana admits that her early childhood had a major role in developing her into who she is today. "Waking up every day and being grateful that you've done so is a gift," she says. In this respect, hardship may have put Oksana through unthinkable pain, but those harsh contours have ultimately fashioned the conditions that contributed to her fulfillment. Oksana insists that she is in no way special. Everyone, she continues, has the potential to use their constraints and circumstances as an accelerant for personal greatness and a deeply meaningful life.

Perceived Constraints

Perceived constraints are the limiting beliefs we take on unconsciously—most often as a result of conditioning—and are a primary reason we so often play it safe.

On the surface, limiting beliefs may appear to be innocuous—just thoughts—but can actually be extremely persistent, insidious, and harmful. These mental anchors weigh us down, keep us living small, and limit our ability to think and act boldly and with agency. Perceived constraints usually show up as:

- Negative beliefs and self-talk

- Unregulated or poorly regulated emotions such as fear of failure or fear of success

- Perfectionism

- Imposter syndrome

- Fixed mindset

- The comparison trap

Jordan Peele, the Oscar-winning filmmaker known for his groundbreaking work in the horror genre, faced his own perceived constraints when he first began to make the transition from comedian to horror film director. Even though his internal compass was pointing him in this new direction, Peele had to face down doubts about his ability to be taken seriously in a genre dominated by conventions. He couldn't help but question whether he could break free from preconceived notions about the kinds of issues and stories Black artists should take on and the kind of movies he could make.

"One question that Black and minority creators often face is, must our stories always be about the struggle against oppression? The answer is a resounding No. The only imperative in

Black stories is the same as non-Black stories—to convey our human struggles. Some of our struggles are with society, but others are with the self, with our families, our communities. All of those are Black stories, too."

Ultimately, Peele overcame some of his self-doubt through action. "I wrote 'Get Out' not necessarily as something to get made," he said in *Entertainment Weekly*. "I wrote it more as something that would be fun to write and something that would help me get better as an artist." That combination of intuition and play, which we talk about elsewhere in the book, was an important strategy for defying expectation, breaking through his perfectionism, and minimizing the significant and very real external constraints that come with a racially charged culture.

Much like Peele, entrepreneur Whitney Wolfe Herd had to confront her own self-doubt and fear of failure, as well as long-standing ideals that society has historically held about women and dating. The CEO and founder of Bumble, the dating app that disrupted the traditional power dynamics of dating, she faced many challenges in a male-dominated industry, which often adhered to traditional gender norms when it came to relationships. Though she knew she wouldn't succeed without pushing back against those external constraints, her primary obstacle was her internal struggle, which she credits as the inspiration for Bumble's unique approach—putting women in control of initiating conversations.

One of the most important aspects of Herd's success is her advocacy for personal authenticity in business. "The greatest rewards often come from the biggest leaps of faith," she told me while emphasizing the importance of embracing vulnerability and turning internal doubts into strengths. And to what does she credit her ability to take these actions and live this life? "Surround yourself with positive, like-minded people who uplift and inspire you." It's through vulnerability and connecting with others in our own authentic way that Herd has flipped the script to inspire and reimagine an entire industry.

Graphic artist, designer, and art director James Victore also wears his vulnerability on his sleeve and tackles many of his internally limiting beliefs out in the open with his artwork, posters, and books. His book titled *Feck Perfuction: Dangerous Ideas on Business and Life* is a perfect example of how to overcome limiting beliefs. According to James, truly excelling in a crowded world requires a commitment to being yourself and tapping into the things that set you apart. Those weird traits, inclinations, and characteristics we're all told to suppress as kids are what give us our unique personalities, and ultimately, our value. "The things that made you weird as a kid," he told me once over tacos, "make you great today."

Environmental Constraints

Environmental constraints are usually the easiest sort of constraints to navigate because they are defined by things within your control, like the place you work, the clutter in your office, your circle of friends. But these constraints are not to be taken lightly, for we tolerate them far too often and then grow accustomed to them, even when they negatively impact our lives or limit our growth.

You *think* you're stuck in that job, with a boss you very much dislike, but the reality is that changing jobs or even switching careers isn't nearly the hurdle you imagine. Your roommate situation? Merely a circumstance you've allowed to persist. The older camera that constrains your success as a photographer? That's just a lie you're telling yourself. None of these problems will solve themselves, but with some action and short-term disruption, they can be managed for the sake of long-term gain.

These types of constraints show up in life usually in the form of:

- Job or career dissatisfaction

- A messy, cluttered, or uninspired living situation

- Financial strain

- An unhealthy lifestyle

Environmental constraints were a huge part of what was holding Scott Harrison back. In the neon world of New York City nightlife, he found himself immersed in a sea of excess and hedonism. Even as the music pulsed, the lights danced, and the Rolex on his wrist informed him that he was regularly not getting to bed until four or five in the morning, he knew something had to change. Despite numerous attempts at stepping back from the underground scene, he always found his way back to a gritty lifestyle of parties, drugs, and superficial friendships with nefarious characters.

Then began the awareness. He described himself as "the worst person he knew." He was teetering between a life that checked all the traditionally accepted boxes—wealth, popularity, a jet-setting career, and fancy vacations—and an existential angst that threatened to consume him. But somehow, after a few scary incidents at one of the clubs he was promoting, he'd finally had enough. After a solo road trip, Scott sold everything he owned and started the next chapter of his life, in tune with the fragility of his existence and with a desire for a legacy other than being "the guy that got a million people wasted."

His soul-searching ultimately led him to a pivotal realization—he needed to find a purpose that transcended the glittering lights of his past. It was during this quest for meaning that Scott volunteered for Mercy Ships, a medical humanitarian mission that opened his eyes to a world he'd never known, where a team of hundreds of volunteers worked tirelessly to help some of the poorest communities on the planet live a better life through education, healthy habits, and lifesaving surgeries. This in turn directed his attention to the global water crisis: how the lack of clean water plagued nearly a billion people in communities worldwide.

In a matter of months, after returning to the States, he was able to raise $97,000 from a gallery show he'd pulled together based on his photos from the experience in Liberia. It was then that he committed to turning away from a life centered on self-indulgence to one centered on serving others. With a resolute spirit, Scott soon founded charity: water, an organization dedicated to bringing clean water to those in need. His mission was clear—to make clean water a basic human right, accessible to every individual on the planet. It was a bold departure from the world of nightclubs and champagne, but Scott's conviction fueled the transformation.

Leveraging his skills in event planning and marketing, Scott orchestrated campaigns that blended creativity with purpose. And through innovative initiatives and radical transparency, he engaged communities and mobilized resources for the cause. His journey marked a shift from a life constrained by a dead-end lifestyle to a purpose-driven existence. And across this process he's emerged as a beacon of change, having today raised more than $750 million that provides nearly 20 million people around the world with clean drinking water.

Too Much of a Good Thing

"How much is enough?" Kate asked me.

It was a confusing moment. I was just out of the shower, standing there in a towel with wet hair, trying hard to make sense of the question. I understood the words, of course, but I didn't have an answer because she'd introduced something so foreign to me—so unthinkable—that my brain simply choked on the input, not unlike when a laptop shows the spinning rainbow of death because the CPU is overloaded. I just couldn't adequately process what she was saying.

A series of career milestones had rapidly come to fruition over the previous several months. My commercial photography was on a hot streak, winning numerous awards for big campaigns and drawing lots of attention for innovation in the space; an iPhone app I'd launched—the first to use photos as the basis for a social network—had gone to number one on the charts and been named App of the Year on the Apple iTunes platform by *MacWorld*, the *New York Times*, and others; an online learning platform I'd started just a year prior was in early talks about being acquired for never-work-again amounts of money; and just an hour before stepping out of that particular shower in the Player's Suite at the newly opened Cosmopolitan Hotel in Las Vegas, I had shared the stage with Lady Gaga and a billionaire to announce that I'd be endorsing Polaroid along with Gaga—the queen of the meat dress at the time—in a relaunch of the iconic camera brand that promised to unite the nostalgia of its past with a new, exciting, digital-first future.

To say I was on a roll would have been an understatement. And as far as I was concerned, this was what winning looked like. My life and my professional accomplishments had transcended even my wildest dreams and were everything that I had been working toward and everything I'd wanted for the past dozen years or more.

Therein lay the problem. I had gone *beyond* what I'd wanted, and I'd lost track of what I truly wanted.

Coming from very humble beginnings, the tidal wave of success seemed like a welcome surprise; however, despite the awards, daily press features, fire hose of money, parties, and newly acquired C-grade celebrity status (mostly by association, if I'm honest)—just a millimeter underneath the surface, our creative studio's mighty little team—myself included—was breaking.

If I was the "talent," then Kate was the business leader. Her health had been on a downward spiral for years due to an undetected endocrine imbalance, serious anxiety, and—I would come to learn later—a significant eating disorder that was taking its toll. The rest of the team traveled constantly, at least a couple of days each week, so they were perpetually sick, missing their kids' birthdays, and working early morning to late-late almost every night even when they were at home. Along with my business manager, I was doing hundreds of thousands of air miles; overnight trips to Shanghai, Tokyo, and London were common. I ate every meal out, I was easily consuming twenty-plus drinks per week, my personal assistants had assistants, and I hadn't set foot in a grocery store or touched a load of laundry in years.

The details might sound tantalizing to some—or like child's play to real celebrity superstars—and I'm not judging either way. But it wasn't for me. Kate knew it, and her question made me realize that deep down, I knew it, too.

On the surface I wore the lifestyle well—always on point in meetings and social media, of course—but inside I was flailing, eagerly stuffing money into anything shiny to deflect the truth of my situation. It wasn't about flashy stuff like fashion and watches for me, but I was definitely torching money and other resources on bicontinental living, startup investments, commercial real estate, ego-padded conveniences, and heavy bets on even more emerging lines of business. I had totally lost sight of myself. What was driving me was simply the near-constant stream of feel-good neurochemicals to my brain.

More was all I really wanted. Just more.

"So how much is enough?" she asked a second time, since I'd stared blankly at her the first time she asked the question a moment earlier. She wasn't being mean or harsh, which made it extra hard to answer. In typical Kate fashion, she had asked it in the most earnest, kindhearted way imaginable.

The confusion I felt initially faded away because I knew exactly what she was getting at. I fumbled to answer, mumbling under my breath from behind the towel I was using to dry my hair. I had no *real* answer because I knew deep down that I was living a lie.

I'd shared with her many times that I really wanted a great lifestyle, but what was important to me was to be an artist with the freedom to do good, creative work. I wanted to spend time—outside whenever possible—with kind, fun, inspiring people. To be a lighthearted anchor in our group of close-knit friends, to volunteer for causes I believed in, to travel the world occasionally as we had done when we were younger. Mostly, I wanted to live the good life tucked up in our tidy little corner of the Pacific Northwest.

That life, however, was very far away from the life we were leading—and even further off from wherever the rocket ship we had built together was on track to take us. I realized in that moment that what used to be "enough," just a short time before, had now become old news. The new answer to how much was enough—how much money, how many friends, how many followers, how many awards—was easy as far as I was concerned. MORE, just *more*.

The truth was that my unconstrained ambition, the pursuit of more for the sake of more, and the complete disregard for any "costs" that might show up in my personal and professional life harmed my health, cost me friends, almost cost me my marriage, and to a certain degree, my life. And this wasn't going to be the last time that in the pursuit of more I risked ending up with less. As I said in the introduction, I had to repeat this pattern a few more times before I finally learned the value of constraints and the other levers.

Ultimately I slowed down and began the process of rejecting

the pursuit of more for more's sake. Over time, I rearranged my priorities in line with my values, putting health and family above career and image, and I developed a set of daily habits that supported this new North Star. And the effects were transformative, expanding my experience of happiness, peace, connection, and impact. Unfortunately, it would just take a decade or so for me to get my wild swings in check between playing it safe and playing by my own rules.

You are likely familiar with the disastrous side effects of hustle culture. "More" is the favorite mantra of hustlers, and bigger and better are the constant aims of those enmeshed in the toxic culture of performance.

As online business leader Jenna Kutcher says, "The problem that I have with hustle culture is that it never ends. There's never enough." And she's right. It never ends. For many of us, it takes a major wake-up call to realize the truth. For Jenna, becoming a mom helped her see how much bigger life could be in the seemingly "small" things like raising a family and attending to her daily tasks as a mom. Most of the time the little stuff in life *is* the big stuff.

Personal finance experts are quick to caution clients to create a conscious spending plan so that they know how they're going to direct their money. But we would be well advised to do the same thing when it comes to building a life. You must develop a budget—a set of constraints to guide your focus, attention, and energy—so that you know when you're overspending. Without these boundaries, it's all too easy to drift into dangerous territory.

All of this makes me think of the breakout 1990s cinematic masterpiece *Free Willy*. In this film, a domesticated killer whale suffers from flaccid fin syndrome, a condition that causes the orca's dorsal fin to drape to one side, which is the result of living in captivity without the resources to adapt to the natural world. Willy is (spoiler alert!) ultimately set free of the limits of his captivity after a series of harrowing, dramatic events.

Humans don't have dorsal fins, of course, but an analogous sort of atrophy *can and will* occur if we live a life that is not laced with challenges or bound by value-driven constraints. If we allow either too much fear or too much comfort or both to stop us from moving forward, over, around, and through the obstacles in our life, we become like an orca with a flaccid fin. The old colloquialism "Use it or lose it" comes to mind. By using constraints to give shape and form to your creativity, you can access both opportunity and growth. Unlike Willy, you have a choice.

Finally, a note on hustling versus challenge. While hustling may seem productive, it's mostly achievement-oriented busyness without much purpose. Challenges, on the other hand, are necessary for opportunity, growth, and evolution. Perhaps you've heard the story of the butterfly working to escape its cocoon. A man sat and watched as it struggled for several hours to break open its chrysalis. Eventually, the insect went still, and the man decided that it must be too tired to continue to fight to get out of the small hole it had made at the end of its shell, so he snipped off the end of the chrysalis with a pair of scissors.

When the butterfly emerged, it had a swollen body and small, shriveled wings. The man continued to watch the butterfly totter around, waiting for it to extend its wings and fly away. But it never did. Without working its way out of the cocoon, its body was hopelessly overloaded with fluid, and its wings were not strong enough to carry it away.

Don't get me wrong—most lives are full of constraints, and we may never need to willingly impose them on ourselves. That may seem depressing on the surface, but on two vectors it's actually quite meaningful. First, a life void of constraints is literally not possible. Second, we ought never seek a life that only aims to minimize constraints, for that would be a life without challenge. This lies in contrast to this entire book. So the next time you think to yourself, how can I make this easier? Think again. Consider if you are avoiding something uncomfortable or if there is a valuable lesson to be learned by facing this difficult experience.

Lever 5

Play

The Most Important Work We Do

In 2018, Novak Djokovic decided to quit tennis. After a series of painful defeats and injuries, he walked away from the game entirely, announcing his plans for retirement to his team. They protested, of course, but he was done. He didn't even want to watch other people play anymore.

Shortly after this, Djokovic and his family went on vacation. Although the tennis pro was burnt-out, his wife, Jelena, still very much loved the game and enjoyed playing it with their young children. So each morning during their trip, she got up to take the kids to the tennis court to play.

Djokovic didn't go.

By the third or fourth day, however—either out of curiosity or boredom—he decided to tag along. As the world-famous athlete watched his wife and children run around the court, chasing balls and laughing, something in him stirred. Seeing the people he loved simply enjoying the game he had dedicated his life to, his stance started to soften. They weren't pushing their bodies to the limit, trying to win at all costs. They were just having a good time.

"Can I have a racket, please?" he asked his wife.

"No," she teased. "You're not playing anymore. You quit tennis, so just leave us the court. Now it's our time."

Then his son Stefan shouted, "Okay, Daddy. It's your turn now!"

Djokovic took the racket, along with a few balls, and started serving. By the end of the day, he had rediscovered a tiny spark of curiosity and joy, the same emotions he once felt as a child during his early years on the court. Fifteen years into his professional career, what had once been fun had become a grind. But with the perspective he gained from stepping back from the sport and the opportunity to witness his family's love for the game, he felt a renewed willingness to play again. After that day, he came to the court every day with his family to play tennis. On the last day of the trip, he told his wife that he was going to call his coach and tell him he was ready to come back.

Djokovic went on to win another dozen grand slams, passing all other players in the history of the game to win a total of twenty-four (at the time of this printing). He is arguably the most talented tennis player in the world right now and nearly walked away for good all because he had forgotten about the joy of play.

We may not be professional tennis players or even the best in the world at what we do, but most of us can relate. Without novelty, fun, connection, and curiosity, anything we love can become work. But what Djokovic's story shows is that no matter who we are and what stage of life we're in, we can go back and work can—by one's choosing—again become play, because play is always fuel for life.

The Cost of Your Comfort

The industrial revolution is generally agreed to have been a big win for human progress—on many levels. It propelled technological innovations that led to unprecedented growth in manufacturing and established the factory as a model of radically efficient production at scale. In turn, the gears and pistons that drove that growth produced a symphony of economic development, resulting in a skyrocketing volume of new jobs, as well as a newfound era of public wealth that was previously unthinkable. The once-quiet array of towns exchanged their gentle hum for the cacophony of urban dreams, and the migration from rural areas to cities fueled social interactions and cultural expansion like never before.

But behind the sprawling factories and rising wages, a different tale simultaneously began to unfold. The life of the worker straddled a gap from opportunity to exploitation and back again. The planet began to take on its first scars of progress, and social structures kicked off a shift that would continue for the next hundred years or more, oscillating, fragmenting, and realigning to changing economic and political tides.

Overall, the accelerating rate of change also brought with it a new uncertainty of where it was all going—both for better and for worse.

It was somewhere around the same time that the human

experience called play began to die a slow death. Play, leisure, and everything associated with fun—for kids and adults alike—began its steady retreat from our daily lives, a retreat that has continued until . . . well, today.

But this is why reengaging with our native experience of play—understanding the inherent joys and the incredible upside it provides—is one of the most important, valuable, and urgent tasks before us. And it turns out that this is another cornerstone that the happiest, most successful and fulfilled people know: play is a massive lever and is an essential part of refusing to "*play*" it safe.

Getting Lost to Find Yourself Again

Let's imagine for a second a "fantasy world" where playing leads to all the same benefits as working does—but even more. In this mythical world, the more we play, the more joy we experience, the more satisfaction we find in our work, the more health benefits we have. And on top of that, we live longer, have better relationships, and feel more connected, happy, and fulfilled. Can you picture it?

Not really? Stay with me here . . .

Now go even deeper to a place where we play for its own sake. Play isn't a means to an end. It's not a necessary break from work that fuels our creativity. It's just something we do with no specific aims. Sure, in some abstract way play might influence any number of other areas of our lives, but we're not playing for any particular reason. We're just following our curiosity and letting our minds wander without any objectives. THAT's the true beauty and freedom of play.

Of all the levers, play is the easiest and the hardest for most adults. We know we need to take breaks, we know we need to rest, but even when we have or make the time, lots of us have completely lost our radar for fun. It's tragic but true. If this resonates for you, do not be afraid, for play is truly a natural state you can return to. I promise. It is a flame that can certainly be dimmed, but it cannot be entirely snuffed out. That said, you really ought to apply effort toward remembering and rekindling it as fast as you can. Don't let another moment go by. By simply *unlearning* and *remembering* what you already know deep inside, by making small adjustments to your thoughts, you can reawaken joy and curiosity and create a gigantic transformation of nearly all your day-to-day experiences. All this is available to you right now. Will you give it a try?

When you were a kid, no one had to teach you to play. You came by it easily and quickly. We all did. But as life moves on, we humans get more serious. We lose touch with our natural ways of being. Our brains calcify; we get locked into certain routines and stop enjoying ourselves as much. We don't want to get anything "wrong," even play. But why? Striving for perfection is when life becomes a grind, relationships start to feel like obligations, and sometimes even getting out of bed becomes a chore. Without joy and curiosity, we lose our way.

Our teachers and parents and mentors taught us this was to be expected, showing us the importance of planning and worrying. We were taught to live in the future, making to-do lists so that we could maximize productivity. Or in the past—thinking over and over of the things we could have done better. And as a result, we tend to rush from one activity to the next, increasingly uptight, quite often unable to let go for just a second. Happiness can feel temporary and fleeting. Whatever accomplishments we earn seem ephemeral. We are lost in a sea of seriousness.

But it doesn't have to be that way.

To live a more meaningful life, you don't need another vacation. You don't need a new hobby or another workout routine. You don't need a constant stream of self-improvement projects. Those things can be helpful, yes, but sometimes they're just one more activity you're piling onto an already overstressed life. What most of us really need is a life we're not trying to escape.

Deep down we need novelty, exhilaration, fun, excitement, and unpredictability in our lives. That's what play is all about and a big part of what made childhood so thrilling. For many of us, this stopped when we became adults. Or, rather, we became adults when we stopped playing.

But it's time to begin to play again.

In his bestselling book *Essentialism*, Greg McKeown writes, "Play doesn't just help us to explore what is essential. It is essential in and of itself." So if we are wise, we understand that play is not a break from what we're doing; it's a dream, a stage, a game, and the very bedrock from which we accomplish anything at all. At the end of the day, play is the secret to a well-lived life.

In a game, there are often two teams who take up two

sides of the field. On the field, there are usually goals, some system to keep score, and a way to acknowledge who has won and lost. But none of this is actually the game. These are just the parameters for the game to be played. The game is what happens between the goals on the field of play. We only need the edges and rules and competitors to help us contain the game itself.

This is an important distinction to acknowledge, as some people think the point of a game is to win. It's not.

In game theory, there are finite games and infinite games, as I mentioned in the discussion on time. Both involve strategic experiments and decision-making, where players aim for objectives. Both types of games have rules and constraints that define their scope, but where they differ is in their endpoints. Finite games have goals in mind, and the game crowns winners when that goal is reached. Infinite games, on the other hand, lack a predetermined endpoint; they continue indefinitely with the goal of playing forever, which requires adaptability. If you grew up reading *Calvin and Hobbes*, Calvinball is the ultimate infinite game. It goes on and on forever, and the only rule is that you can never play it the same way twice. Like Calvin and Hobbes, if you're playing an infinite game, you have to think on your feet and be willing to flex on strategies, experiments, and play as the game evolves.

I am reminded of what I consider the epitome of play and an example I love so much that I also wrote about it in *Creative Calling*. When author and marketing expert Seth Godin was a boy, his mom would get fed up with a house full of kids on days when school wasn't in session, so she would drop Seth and his friends off at Sheridan Lanes, down the road from his house, for a few hours of bowling. Since time was limited, and it cost money to bowl, they could only count on a few games. Every roll of the ball mattered, and they didn't feel good about wasting even one. So Seth imagined a new game he called unlimited or infinite bowling.

> *Unlimited bowling is a whole different concept. . . . Roll to your heart's content. When you're doing unlimited bowling, you can practice various shots. You can work on the risky splits. You can bowl without remorse. Interesting is enough. Generous is enough. Learning is enough. . . . It's a special kind of freedom and we shouldn't waste it.*

Consider if we approached life the same way.

In Hinduism, there is a word to describe this phenomenon as it pertains to life, and it's called *lila*, which means divine play. *Lila* is the dance between opposing sides in life, a way to bring harmony to seemingly all aspects of life, such as victory and struggle, pain and ecstasy, even birth and death. In the game of life, where everything seems so serious, what can we do with all these rules and impossibly high stakes? Rather than retreat into a metaphorical shell, or fall in lockstep with all the other serious, boring, dull, and bottled-up adults, what if you took a chance at a different experience? What if you saw that play is fuel for life? Like the creativity that makes it possible, what if play was not a nice-to-have addition to an already full life, but instead the cornerstone of all your waking moments and virtually everything you do? Seem extreme? It's not, and here's why.

The Shit That Leads to Play

During the coronavirus pandemic, my wife and I split our time between our home in Seattle and a cabin up the coast that's been in the family for decades. Over time, the beach house has become more than a second home to us—it's a refuge of sorts, and we ended up buying the property from my parents and starting to make it our own.

One weekend, shortly after acquiring the house, I drove up for a solo trip to take a look around. This was just after I'd transitioned out of my role as CEO of CreativeLive. My free time was abundant, but the strangeness of the pandemic had descended, and, like everyone during that odd, scary time, my life was full of questions.

Who was I now?

What was the rest of life going to look like?

Would I ever have another project as big and impactful as my last company?

For weeks, I had tried to think my way through these questions. But no amount of intellectual thrashing made the slightest difference. This was the impetus to make the ninety-minute drive up the coast to visit the cabin. That first night, I tossed and turned, unable to sleep. The next day I woke up early, and for some reason and without any advance planning, I decided to undertake the most annoying, least glamorous task I could think of. I dug up my own shitbox. *Literally*.

Shitbox is a term I'd learned from my surly old neighbor, Marvin. It's the moniker he used to describe the septic system, which is the more formal name for a series of underground components that treat wastewater on-site, most commonly in rural areas without a municipal sewer system. Any internet search will return a host of polite names for these systems, including domestic wastewater systems, individual sewage systems, and residential wastewater treatment systems, among others. But Marvin wasn't having it—a shitbox was a shitbox, pure and simple.

So I called it what he did—more to the point, I figured.

Out of curiosity, I'd asked my parents the last time they'd serviced the septic system, and they couldn't remember. Not a good sign. I started investigating, asking around to find out what the neighbors knew. They told us to hire a professional, but I wasn't so sure that was the next right step. My gut told me it was worth looking into on my own first.

Normally these systems have clearly designated access points that are visible from the surface, somewhere tucked in the corner of the yard. But not ours. Those access points, wherever they were, had gotten fully buried by shifting dirt levels and rains over the years. But seventy-five-year old Marvin had lived nearby since he was a kid and had memories of my great-uncle John installing the system. He gave me a hint about where the access points might be. As a lifelong tinkerer, and with a little ornery direction from Marvin, I decided to give the project a whirl. I would dig up the system myself and make sure everything was in order.

From the moment I started, I traveled back in time to playing in the yard as a kid. My parents had built all the homes we'd ever lived in, so I knew my way around a construction site. Just the thought of digging in the dirt sounded fun. Which it was. Rubber boots, shovels, and gloves. Dirt clods and big piles of sticky mud. Although it wasn't easy and required a good bit of physical effort to spoon all the earth from one place to another, I made the digging process a game.

It was incredibly joyful and satisfying, despite a sweaty brow.

And as various neighbors walked by with their dogs, they'd stop and ask about my project. We'd laugh and swap a few lighthearted stories about projects they'd tackled themselves, for better or for worse.

Time flew by.

After what turned out to be an entire summer day of getting my hands dirty—literally—I uncovered the main tank. Then, after a bit more internet research, and a few in-person professional opinions, I discovered that the system was actually in good shape. Thank you, Great Uncle John. "Existing and performing, nonconforming" was how it was categorized. All the system needed was a new lid. So instead of hiring a team to replace the entire septic system, which would have cost us at least $50,000, I commissioned my brother-in-law, Jack, who is a talented blacksmith, to fabricate a new, custom steel lid for a few hundred bucks.

That lid felt like a work of art to me. I had a blast sketching up the details on graph paper before sharing my designs with a few of the online communities I discovered while researching—I'd actually made a few internet friends in the process. A little elbow grease, some design work, a whole lot of tinkering, and voila—project complete.

What a rush.

Tongue-in-cheek, of course, but I did think of this all as a fun little game. I played. I lost track of time, I engaged others, experimented, got dirty, and learned. What could have been an embarrassing, awkward, er . . . shitty pile of "work" was transformed by a hunch and an intention.

You might think this is where the story ends, but it does not. Encouraged by my rediscovered joy, I decided to see what else I could tinker with the following weekend, moving on to the poorly draining garbage disposal. After a few minutes of pulling it apart, I was flooded by memories of working on cars as a kid with my dad, changing the air filters and oil.

Again, nostalgia and joy. The tools felt like toys. I called a buddy I hadn't spoken to in months for advice, because he's a lovely human and one of those guys who can fix anything. He helped me solve my problem in minutes once I'd fiddled with a few nuts and bolts.

Next, I moved on to tightening our kitchen cabinet doors, which had fallen slightly out of alignment over the years. Some sagged just enough to miss their magnetic latches. Others squeaked. I had to pick up a few more "toys" at the hardware store, learn a few more things online, and borrow some stuff from Alan the neighbor to make it happen. But what a joy it all was.

After that, I hung a few pieces of art.

Then rewired the power to the pilot light for the gas stove.

It was all a game, and I loved it. None of these repairs were revolutionary. I can't emphasize this enough. These were just everyday tasks that needed to be done. But tackling them as play to be embraced, rather than as chores, opened up a flow in me that had been dormant for months.

By Sunday night, I had plowed through a half-dozen other

small projects, and although I'd worked a couple of twelve-hour days, I felt a strange surge of energy. I made several trips from the city to the beach and back over the next few weeks to continue my *play*. My mind hadn't felt that clear and uncluttered—I would describe it as "at ease"—in several months.

This would continue—from reengaging with my writing habit to birth the book you're reading right now to remodeling my old photo studio to starting golf lessons after a twenty-year hiatus. Even my "chores" felt different than they had before my mindset shift—all of which was kicked off by merely tinkering around and getting into some . . . shit.

All of a sudden, I was *playing* at life again, and it was unmistakably affecting everything for the better. Energy, joy, novelty. Levity and presence. Learning, laughing, and exercising my brain. As a guy who'd grown up playing sports, who'd ditched the traditional career path to live as an action sports photographer playing in the outdoors with friends, and who had wobbled a bit on my values to go hard-core into business where hundreds of millions of dollars were at stake and I'd gotten a little lost in the process, I had found my way back home on the wings of playing in my yard. Standing on the new lid for my septic tank felt better—funnier and more fun—than any red carpet or private jet.

In Case You Needed Proof

The research from Stuart Brown's National Institute for Play is clear: "Imagination is the source of every form of human achievement . . . and it's the one thing I believe we are systematically jeopardizing in the way we educate our children and ourselves."

Dr. Brown suggests that playing is really practice for life, and the better we play, the better we will be at living. He argues that to deprive oneself of play is to live only half a life. In fact, he points to an abundance of data that indicates such deprivation can lead to an underdeveloped brain.

In one study, for example, Brown tracked the play patterns of cats, showing that when they don't learn to play, they fail to become properly socialized. They still learn to hunt, but they don't know how to be around other cats, often viewing them as enemies and attacking them. This is similar to rats and other social mammals, he says—even humans. We may not need play for the basic aspects of survival, but we certainly need it to make the most of a life. Without it, our species would adapt at a slower rate, and our world would tend to feel very small and threatening.

But aside from the reasons we *need* play, it also teaches you to enjoy life, to not see everything as a constant competition but rather as one long game filled with opportunity. Unfortunately, our go-go culture has pushed play aside, rendering many of us poorly prepared for the world. In the book *Play*, Brown writes, "students today will face work that requires much more initiative and creativity than the rote work that the current educational approach was designed to prepare them for. In a sense, they are being prepared for twentieth-century work, assembly-line work, in which workers don't have to be creative or smart—they just have to be able to put their assigned bolt in the assigned hole."

Unsurprisingly, this way of being is already verifiably out-dated. Considering how fast information moves today and how that translates to accelerating rates of change, we literally *need* play to help us keep up. As a scientifically proven booster to plasticity in the brain, play functions to enhance the brain's neural networks to adapt and reorganize, effectively rewiring them to function in new, adaptive ways that depart from old ways of operating. In short, it helps us evolve and is therefore not just a "nice-to-have," like an ice cream cone as a follow-on to a Philly cheesesteak lunch.

In the anthropological work of Johan Huizinga and Brian Sutton-Smith, we learn that play isn't just recreation or merely a game; it's also a vibrant thread that weaves us together through social development. In Huizinga's masterwork, *Homo Ludens*, he invites us to reimagine play as a ceremonial act that "reveals human's natural wiring for play as a ritualistic force," shaping norms and nurturing identities. He goes far beyond play as simply "fun" to instead align play as a much more integrated, cultural phenomenon—a fundamental aspect of the culture that influences how societies convene and relate to themselves and one another. Sutton-Smith's work broadens these ideas to include the creative, the imaginative, and the everyday. It's as if "play itself is a language" through which we communicate our values, traditions, and shared norms.

In a more abstract but interesting point of view, philoso-pher, poet, and playwright Friedrich Schiller posited a "play drive" that made it possible to acquire freedom of thought and fulfill our potential. In his research and writings, the play drive fuses the demands of our "sensuous materiality" where we are bound up in time and nature (our "sense drive") with the demands of our reason, or our need to shape things (our "form drive"). And it is only play he deems that can reconcile these two existential poles. As humans, he professes, we have a foot each in being and becoming, and play is what allows us to dance with both.

In short, to return for a moment to Dr. Stuart Brown's research, "nothing lights up the brain like play."

If you're at all like me, when I can be still enough to hear what's true for me—all this research matches the personal and empirical evidence I've witnessed across my lifetime. I'm at my best when the world is a lighthearted game, and the consequences are limited—whether alone or with friends, at work or home. That's not to say, of course, that there aren't places to be serious and focused (more on that later). But I can say with confidence that a person's success and happiness are tied largely to their ability to recreate well—their playfulness. I've seen this in the lives of many of my happiest friends and many of the world's most fulfilled individuals, and it's true for me as well. The more we play, the better we feel. The better we feel, the more open we are to the moment. And the more open we are to the moment, the more we can experience a richer humanity, better relationships, and better lives.

Learning to Play It Away

Charlie Hoehn graduated from college in 2008, and like a lot of his friends, he expected things to fall into place. They didn't. Charlie spent his first few months as a graduate applying for jobs on CareerBuilder, Craigslist, and other similar platforms—with no luck.

Having sunk his time and energy into college, Charlie wondered what the point was. His mom told him that she thought it would be a good idea to go back to school and get an MBA, since no one was hiring at the time. But Charlie knew another degree wasn't the answer. He wanted to get out in the world and explore.

Charlie's plan was to spend the next few months working with people he really admired, for free if he had to, just to see what he might gain from real-world experience. If anything positive came of it, great. Maybe he could create the job he wanted instead of waiting for someone to give it to him. And if it didn't work out, he'd be back to where he started. Then he might consider grad school or continuing the job search. It was just an experiment, and there was no way to lose.

First, Charlie signed up for a virtual internship with a legendary business and marketing specialist. So did many other people, *but* at the end of the internship, only about a dozen of the original two hundred interns had stuck with it, so his "boss" promoted these people on his blog. This led to multiple job offers for Charlie, and he ended up working with none other than Tim Ferriss. During his time working with Tim, Charlie helped plan events, launch books, and more. The work was demanding for a twenty-four-year-old college grad, but it was also an invaluable opportunity.

Leading up to a VIP event Charlie was helping plan for Tim—which, incidentally, is where I first met Charlie in person—his life had become a never-ending series of caffeinated drinks, catnaps, and running from one thing to the next. The stress became nearly unbearable, but there was no one else to do the work. So he kept doing it.

Charlie knew that if he didn't do a stellar job on the project, it might mean the end of a career that had only just begun. To keep up with the demands of his work, he ordered some "smart drugs" from a pharmaceutical company overseas. These were stimulants that had been designed for fighter pilots to stay awake for multiday missions. Charlie ended up staying up for four days straight so that if anything went wrong he'd be awake to fix it. Over the course of a week, he slept a total of six hours.

After the event, it was more of the same. He kept pushing himself harder and harder. Next up was a new book project for Tim, which meant more long days and a demanding schedule. But something started to feel off. "I knew the ride in front of me," he recalled, "and didn't know if I was gonna make it."

Around that same time, Charlie had a family member pass away as well as a close friend attempt suicide. The deadline for the book was pushed back six months, so he decided to use the pause to take a week off and figure out what was next. When he returned to work, Charlie told his boss it was time to quit. He was shaking the whole time. "I was just toast," he told me later. After that, he spent a season "spinning out and trying to figure out what was going on." He'd never felt this way before in his life and didn't understand it. Eventually, it would be diagnosed as anxiety.

Like any problem, Charlie figured he could just power through it, but when that didn't work, he saw his doctor, who prescribed a bunch of meds. After that, he tried yoga, meditation, therapy, journaling, extreme diets, intense exercise, and just about every supplement and medication you can think of. He volunteered, prayed, used float tanks, even experimented with psychedelics. None of it really did the trick.

When he was at his wits' end, a friend recommended Stuart Brown's book on the power of play. Human beings, he learned, can be denied a lot in life. They can go weeks without eating, days without water, even years without work. But, he concluded, "human beings are designed to play."

Charlie decided to undergo a thirty-day experiment of playing every single day. He went on mini-adventures, tried his hand at improv, took daily walks, worked on puzzles. He even purchased a bucketful of baseballs and a bat and took to meeting his friend at a nearby park that was seldom used by others, where they'd trade off pitching to each other and smashing balls around the empty field. He'd loved baseball as a kid. This simple exercise from his past brought immeasurable joy and kneecapped his anxiety in a way that was more effective—and healthier—than the antianxiety drugs he's tried before.

In the end, Charlie faced his own workaholism and addiction to status. He learned to relax and enjoy himself instead of acting as if the next milestone was the "big one." By the end of the experiment, he had no symptoms of anxiety. "I just felt normal again," he told me. "I realized that play utterly destroys anxiety."

Based on the science and our human experience, play isn't just about *feeling* better—although that's an amazing outcome by itself. When seen through a broader, more accurate, and inclusive lens, play *makes everything* better.

Play First, Work Second

So let's get down to brass tacks.

We all understand that play is fun and easy, but that's partly because we're also conditioned from an early age to think it is limited, frivolous, and a recreational luxury only for *after* work is done.

The hard division of work and play is drilled into us before we even get out of the starting gates. Case in point: my second-grade teacher, Ms. Kelly! She actually talked me into giving up on my magic shows, my comic strips, and my stand-up comedy act to focus on more serious stuff! Second grade!

Even as adults we reinforce this lie for ourselves. We subscribe to the work hard, play hard mantra. Work is "hard," serious, driven, and compelled, whereas play comes only after the work is done.

"You can play later, first do your chores," our guardians and authority figures say. "Come on, now, get to work, playtime is over."

But what if we flipped the script? What if we played first and worked second? Sure, work is tough, but it leads to progress. But play is fun and leads to whimsy. It ultimately behaves—beyond childhood—as a circuit breaker that allows us to revive and rest, for mental health, for our general well-being.

We live in a culture that celebrates work and moderates play, so it's no wonder you lack leverage in this area of your life. Give yourself a bit of a break.

And then consider for a moment—or rather *remember*—that play has always been a natural state within you. It's not an external language that needs learning, it's an internal capacity that needs reawakening. As a toddler, you didn't have to learn to play before giggling and squirming about. Play was as natural to you as it is to my golden retriever puppy, who incessantly chases his own tail. That should be refreshing news, because if you're in the state I'm guessing you're in—if you're at all like 95 percent of the people I know—your *play* skills have simply lapsed a bit. It's a muscle that you've always had, but it's just atrophied. Fear not, however, because just as our creativity gets trained out of us from an early age, can go dormant, and fully return as a powerful force, so can your drive for fun. That instinctual levity, presence, novelty, connection, and joy.

As Dr. Joe Dispenza reminds us: "95% of who we are by the time we're 35 years old is a set of unconscious automatic programs that we've practiced so many times that we're not consciously thinking. The first step is: You [must] become conscious of your unconscious thoughts."

So now that you're conscious, you must act. Let's go.

Big Magic

We all know and love the state of flow when whatever task is at hand just seems easy and effortless. The words and ideas just keep coming, and all we have to do is enjoy the process. Elizabeth Gilbert calls this "big magic," citing countless incidents of the spiritual nature of creative and playful work. To be sure, there are inexplicable moments of profound inspiration that seem to channel from some otherworldly place. And, in my experience, this is not a state to be wished for. It is something we can create.

For centuries, creators of all types have had to use certain tools and tricks to put themselves into a state of mind that made them ready to engage. Often, these habits were as eccentric as the individuals themselves who practiced them, such as Henry David Thoreau's daily four-hour walk. For him this was a necessity, not a luxury, the baseline of inner focus for him to maintain a sense of peace, presence, and connection to his work.

Or take thriller novelist Patricia Highsmith, who used to sit on her bed surrounded by her cigarettes, ashtray, cup of coffee, donut, and some sugar in preparation for the day's writing. The idea was to remove as much discipline from the process as possible, making writing something so playful that it no longer intimidated her. Then, she could start.

The concept of *flow* is generally understood by most people to be an uncommon, playful, joyful, aware state achieved by the lucky—or by high performers who know their own flow triggers and then meticulously design their lives to achieve this state of heightened motivation, creativity, learning, and well-being. But just like creativity, flow and its close cousin play are available to everyone.

I'd be over the moon to learn that this chapter has you playing in every obvious way possible: running after wake-up, crossword puzzles at breakfast, creating at work, basketball at lunch, theater group after work, experimental cooking for dinner, drinking games for dessert, and good sex before bed. That would certainly be a meaningful shift for most of us seeking the health and happiness benefits of play. That would be amazing.

And yet, my mission would be incomplete if you were not *also* able to substantially shift your thinking about "work" in general after you read this book. When I say work, yes, I mean: your job, your chores, difficult tasks and problems that you must solve—whether personal, professional, spiritual, or otherwise. All of it. Like all of these levers, they only get *really* interesting when you apply pressure on them in ways you'd previously not imagined.

So, what if all that work I listed above brought you joy and presence? What if you even stopped calling it work? What if washing the dishes was a game? Interacting with your toxic boss, or navigating rush-hour traffic? Does it seem too good to be true? If so, I'll leave you with one final "assignment" in this chapter.

Another Tiny Experiment

The reason work becomes work is our orientation toward it. We are conditioned to think of work as unpleasant, the exact opposite of pleasure and play. So ultimately, it's not about shifting the content of what you're doing, it's about shifting the perception of the tasks we have to accomplish every day.

Let's take a task that one might label as a chore, say folding a load of laundry that's just come out of the dryer. (And FWIW, I really do want you to do this the next time you have the chance! You will be amazed.)

If you're like me, this was a chore I had as a young person, and I learned to despise it. It was always something that I wedged in between more desirable activities. I saw it as a task imposed upon me despite the very real outside pressure to not wear a shirt with more wrinkles than a 90 year old man. *This is a waste of time*, I would hear in my head. *Who needs to fold this stuff when I could just jam it in my drawer and nobody would know? Who cares if my pants have wrinkles? I'm so bad at folding these clothes* and so on. I would rather have been doing quite literally anything else.

So the assignment is this: fold the laundry and only fold the laundry. Any time your attention strays—and it will, I promise—simply notice this and redirect your attention to the laundry as perceived through one of the senses.

Now, the next time you hear the buzzer on the dryer and it's time to fetch the clothes and fold them, your plan is clear. First, notice that buzzer—really hear it—and be grateful for a device that is smart enough to notify you when it's done working on your behalf. Next, walk up to the dryer and open it. Feel the warm air on your face as the heat escapes. And listen to the sound—the cute little creaking sound of the dryer door. Smell the pleasant, clean smell—a combo of detergent and dryer sheet. Mmmmm. Reach your hands into the dryer and grab all the clothes, while paying special attention to the soft feeling of the fabric and, again, the warmth. Notice all the colors in the pile, some bright, others faded. Really be here for the folding experience. Have fun with it.

Whoops—thought about when dinner's going to be ready? No big deal. Simply direct your attention back to the feeling of the clothes. With each movement, keep your attention on one of your senses and notice what it's like to interact with the laundry. Maybe dance with a long-sleeve shirt or two. Smell the smells again. Feel the fibers. Chuckle at how absurd it is that we can be shocked by our socks. A little more gratitude sprinkled in there too is nice. Gratitude that you have a dryer to use if you do, that you have clothes, and that you are taking time to be present.

Okay. That's it.

You have just completed a task—something you'd previously dreaded or at least assigned a negative value to: work, negativity, pain, or anger, and you just had somewhere between an entirely neutral to a massively positive experience with it. Joy, play, connection, and presence.

And here's the cool thing. You can do this with almost everything in your life, all the time. Bad traffic? Go to each of your senses, in turn. Remember—it's not what you *think* about what you're hearing, seeing, or feeling emotionally—but only what you're *sensing*. The leather of the steering wheel, the breeze entering the partially opened window, the smell of the sea nearby, the low hum of tires moving slowly on the pavement. Gratitude that you're not having to walk all the way to the city from your house . . . and on and on. How joyful that someone built this car for you! This activity, or "game," to double down on our play theme for a moment, works with *anything* and has the power to reshape your entire world.

Alan Watts talks similarly about washing dishes:

[Y]ou turn the cleaning movement into a dance. Shwww, shwww, shwww, shwww, like this. And you dig that. And you swing that plate around and you let the rinsing water go over it, and you put it off in the rack. Tsk! Crazy. See? Take the next one. Shwww, shwww, shwww, shwww, and you get this rhythm going, see? And you're not under compulsion all the time. . . .

He concludes the monologue by making the point that this is always available to us and that we ought to do everything—literally everything—in this spirit. "Don't make a distinction between work and play," he said. "Regard everything that you are doing as play, and don't imagine for one minute that you've got to be serious about it."

Buddhists call this awareness practice, because all you're doing with each turn of the senses is directing your attention with kindness and using it as a lever to be here in the present moment with whatever you are experiencing without judgment. For, without any exaggeration, this moment is all we have. The past never returns and the future never arrives. We are right here, right now.

To exist in the present moment, in a state of awareness and gratitude, emanating joy may seem like a reach, but this truly is your natural state. Just watch a skillful kindergarten teacher ask their class of students to help clean up the room. Most often there aren't any groans of resistance or whimpers of sadness. On the contrary, the students will more likely dance around, singing a joyful tune about picking up crayons as they perform the requested task. This is *their* natural state. Their next task is likely every bit as joyful as the cleaning, as was the task that preceded it—all of which they're not even thinking about because they are so focused on the present moment.

Could this soon be you?

Lever 6

Failure

A Feature, Not a Bug

Melissa Arnot Reid lay awake in her tent at 17,590 feet above sea level, quietly crying. She wasn't upset because of the harsh conditions at Mount Everest's base camp—she was well acquainted with those. It wasn't fear or anxiety either. *These* were tears of rejection.

Melissa had overheard climbers in an adjacent tent talking about her, wondering why she was trying *again* to summit Everest without oxygen. During the past century, approximately 6,600 people have reached the top, but only about 220 have done it without oxygen. That's a total of 220 humans—since time began—who have accomplished the feat that she was currently attempting. Melissa had already climbed the world's tallest peak twice before *with* oxygen, but she'd also tried and failed, more than once, to summit without it. Those who attempt this feat are exponentially more likely to suffer severe consequences, including death, few are brave enough to give it a shot, let alone more than once.

At this exact moment, however, Melissa wasn't thinking about boldness. She was listening to her peers insinuate that this latest attempt was a fool's errand, and she was unfit for the task. Their words, combined with her own self-doubt, were starting to get to her. Why *was* she trying again when she'd already attempted such an incredibly difficult task and fallen short? Was it true that the mountaineering community had thrown in the towel on her? What would her corporate sponsors think if she failed *again* and demonstrated once and for all that she lacked the chops to tackle this holy grail?

"There were more people who didn't believe in me than who did," she recalled to me.

It was precisely then that Melissa decided she'd had enough.

She didn't stop climbing that day. She didn't quit attempting the near impossible. Instead, what she *did* quit was expecting others to understand and support her unconditionally. She stopped telling so many people her plans and moved to a quieter side of the mountain where she could focus attention and time on her goal without the distraction of outside voices.

Her strategy worked. Even though it took five attempts—*five*—she finally summited Mount Everest and returned to base camp without the assistance of oxygen in 2016—the first American woman to accomplish such a feat.

Few of us will climb Everest, but everyone who reads this sentence has failed before—and will fail a little bit every day until they die.

What that looks like for each of us is different—if you're a perfectionist, it might mean forgetting a few items on the grocery list. If you're a founder, it could be blowing through ten million dollars of investor capital on an idea that doesn't work. Getting dropped by customers. Or your spouse. A car accident that was all your fault, a kid having trouble reading in school, or a million other things that don't go according to plan and awaken that all-too-familiar voice in your head of shame, disappointment, anger, fear—or all of the above.

For most people, however, failure isn't a matter of life and death like it is for Melissa. As a professional mountain climber, she puts her life on the line most days at work, and she often has to make the call *not* to push for the summit when guiding others up icy peaks, despite an immense amount of training—months or even years of preparation in some cases—as well as the big dollars at stake that some of her clients pay her to help them fulfill a dream. The willingness to abort a summit attempt due to unsafe weather or other conditions—essentially admitting failure without in some cases even being able to *attempt* the final leg of the journey—has taught her a lot.

Ironically, I gleaned all this wisdom from Melissa in a very strange location. We were having our first of many discussions about failure on a steep snowfield, somewhere around 19,500 feet above sea level on our final push to summit Africa's highest peak: Mount Kilimanjaro.

In between my huffing and puffing and lots of slow, uphill walking, I learned from Melissa that all her experience in high, dangerous places had taught her to treat failure as a common, albeit strategic part of her life. Her goal, she told me, was to always learn and improve. It was all about small debriefs after mistakes and pressing on again, with a new kernel of knowledge and a positive attitude. And it wasn't just about avoiding mistakes either, she told me. Mistakes happen. But what she made clear to me that day above the clouds was that living humbly in the face of Mother Nature, that learning, and recovering as quickly as possible from the mistakes that she does make—all while attempting to stay even keeled—had given her what she called "a special perspective" toward life.

Melissa has climbed some of the tallest and most dangerous mountains in the world. In addition to all her Everest expeditions, she's seen numerous ascents of Kilimanjaro, Aconcagua, Cotopaxi, and Denali—on her own and as a guide—including having summited Mount Rainier more than ninety times. She's literally stood atop of the world, having done what most could only ever dream about. While she's honest that none of it was easy, as a person who is constantly creating and shaping her own life, she knows something critical: *Without failure, there is no success.*

One lesson she shared with me really stood out. When she faces a big challenge, she replaces the word *fail* with the word *live.* So when she catches herself saying, "I'm afraid to fail," she flips the script and turns it into "I'm afraid to live." This becomes an instant reminder that there is no other way. To live is to fail. Over and over again.

"You know, Chase," she said, breathing seemingly normally, high on the side of Kilimanjaro, while I struggled to sip what felt like the tiniest bits of oxygen out of the alpine air. "All of us, we're not going to succeed at most of the things we try. And forgetting or ignoring this is what keeps so many people from reaching their true potential. Most people just don't have a healthy relationship with failure."

I paused for a moment between agonizingly slow steps and squinted in her direction, thinking that this was a funny moment for her to be giving me this advice. Sweat beaded on my brow, and she pulled out of line behind me to pass, on her way to check in with a few others in our party just ahead of us on the route.

"The good stuff in life doesn't come from success, the good stuff comes from failing."

She smiled and playfully nudged me as she walked by, making it clear that she was simultaneously jesting—since she was all but certain we would be summiting shortly up ahead—but also as serious as a heart attack in making the point that most of us miss: *The good stuff comes from failing.*

So what is the good stuff of failure and how *do* we develop a healthy relationship with all the good and the bad? How can we learn to work with failure in a healthy way, leveraging the benefits of failure, while mitigating the amount of pain we feel in the process?

The Stigma of Failure

"Every winner begins as a loser," says Dashun Wang, professor of management and organizations at Northwestern's Kellogg School of Management, "but not every failure leads to success."

Wang and his colleagues have spent thirty years analyzing data—from venture capital outcomes to grant applications to terrorist attacks and beyond—all in order to better understand the nature of failure. Their results are simultaneously surprising and clarifying. In short, the *try and try again* mantra doesn't work. Instead, it turns out that understanding *how* you failed and reflecting systematically—but not overthinking—about what you can learn and how you can change things for your next attempt is what truly matters.

"The people who ultimately failed [and quit] didn't necessarily work less. They could have actually worked more; it's just that they made more unnecessary changes." In other words, the individuals and groups that persevered more often employed structured frameworks to support their repeated efforts. The guidelines weren't always expressly scientific, but there were rudimentary methodologies to their failures and subsequent attempts. In other words, they had a bit of a plan. They were intentional. They reviewed their failures and specifically avoided "thrashing around and changing everything," according to Wang.

One vector that predicted success was speed. In the case of the grant applicants, for example, it became clear that the faster they recovered from failures—that is, how fast they failed, made a surgical adjustment, and then tried again—the more likely their success. So, the "fail fast" cliché is not entirely correct either. It's not how quickly you fail but rather how quickly you recover with a new, demonstrably different attempt at the solution that matters most.

Trying all sorts of solutions in a ramshackle fashion rarely unlocks the results we're after. It's in studying some aspect of what didn't go well and making a change that we experience improved results.

In the case of trying to beat the boss at the end of a video game, for example, you wouldn't just randomly press buttons on the controller and move the joystick around when faced with the big challenge; you'd pause briefly after the last time you lost, consider what worked and what didn't, and prepare a new plan that leverages your experience *and* a few hunches about what might work going forward. Then you jump back right in the fight. The more familiar you are with all the moves that worked and the more quickly you can run new experiments in rapid succession, the more likely you are to win.

To put it another way, you'd keep changing your angle of attack a little bit and you'd keep going so that wisdom and previous experiences were more likely to compound, until you triumphed. On the merits, the researchers at Northwestern concluded there's an element of calculated momentum that helps winners win and keeps losers losing.

I'm guessing very little of this is a surprise. It's either something you already know, or if it's new to you, it probably makes perfect sense.

But why then is failure so culturally stigmatized? Why, when we watch someone fail at work, or school, or on the playground, do we cringe? Or in the case of our own experiences, why do we feel guilt or shame or anger—perhaps all three—when we stumble? There are a couple of key factors to consider.

First, we are social animals, and we are biologically wired to want to fit into our tribe. So it's understandable that this same wiring fires off a fear response when we fail or make mistakes: failure puts us at risk of getting kicked out of wherever we're trying to belong. And because we fear the possibility of crashing and burning ourselves, we can't help but feel afraid when we see others do the same.

Even though the prospect of looking good if we *do* happen to pull something off—whatever we're attempting to do while avoiding failure—exists, our excitement over that prospect gets throttled down. Sure, we'd like to stand out, so we'll be more acceptable to our tribe, but our biology is simultaneously more geared toward limiting our exposure to mistakes. It's no wonder we're more often content living with the status quo rather than risking the potential downfall or even a stumble that could challenge our place in the pecking order.

The second point, although it's still related to our evolutionary biology, might hit a little closer to home. Our society has transformed so quickly over the past century—and at an ever-accelerating rate—that despite all the information that's available to us, we are today unable to see the work and the repetitions that lead to the vast majority of "success" stories. Media in general, and social media in particular, is masterful at leaving out all the stumbles that were a much more visible part of life when we lived in tribes and villages and smaller domains; instead we see seemingly uninterrupted leaps and bounds. So many people are doing so much epic shit with seemingly little effort or pain that when we compare ourselves, we have no choice but to feel scared to fail.

Not that long ago, struggle was a regular part of human experience, and we witnessed it with our own eyes. We may have heard about a mythic hero from the neighboring village, but what we saw in our day-to-day lives was incremental growth and the systematic, strategic overcoming of obstacles in a natural, human progression. Back then, we were witness to the stumbles and the successes, and they made sense to our brains, whereas today, social feeds showcase curated and often unrealistic visions of success. All this in turn creates an illusion that success should come quickly and easily. Effortless brilliance has become the latest epidemic of false promises. It's no wonder failures show up in our psyches as personal flaws rather than opportunities for growth. Our misunderstandings about failure seem to be at an all-time high and rising.

Living = Meaningful Failure

If we are looking to create the life of our dreams—one where from our deathbed we can exclaim *No regrets!*—then it stands to reason that we ought to see each failure for what it is: a required stepping-stone and a necessary ingredient of fulfill-ment. There is no growth without challenge.

But what all this science and rationalism fails to acknowledge is that failure fucking hurts.

Failure feels absolutely awful in the body and the mind. Maybe the late-for-the-dentist sort of failure doesn't *hurt* per se, or perhaps even the made-a-mistake-that-cost-me-some-money sort of failure isn't truly *painful* in the classic sense of the word. Those failures land just a touch above inconvenient. But let's be real: classic failures at work, in our relationships, or even self-betrayal—these almost always hurt deeply, and some of these mistakes can have real consequences.

Imagine, if you can, the horror of the team at Morton

Thiokol, maker of the booster rockets and O-rings that failed and caused the 1986 Space Shuttle Challenger disaster. Or even failures when no one died, but when those involved might have felt like dying in the moment—like when the host of the Miss Universe Pageant, Steve Harvey, mistakenly announced the wrong winner during the 2015 pageant. After misreading the card, he accidentally crowned Miss Colombia the winner, only to later correct himself and declare Miss Philippines the actual winner. The awkwardness of the situation, coupled with the contestants' reactions, spawned numerous memes and jokes around the world, making it one of the most memorable pop culture fails in recent history. But neither Steve nor Miss Colombia was laughing.

Failures on this level truly hurt. They hurt in the head, heart, and gut. Like a smack upside the skull or a body blow, the experience most people report from meaningful failure is one of real pain at a deep level.

Juxtapose this if you will with trendy bullshit running rampant today saying failure is "no big deal." *I love failure. Failing is fun. Fail fast, fail often! Embrace it and you'll never feel shame again!*

I call this "fail-washing." In the abstract, it sounds like a reasonable reframe, but it's little more than a toxic attempt to minimize and simplify the concept of failure and results in a head-in-the-sand relationship with its real impact. Tell all that garbage to Steve Harvey or the space shuttle team. Because when failure happens to you—when you're in the middle of the mess—all those platitudes are no comfort at all.

So what is the definitive approach to managing failure?

It just so happens that Melissa Arnot Reid was right, along with so many others who refuse to live a small life: there *is* a sweet spot in our relationship to failure where we maximize the best parts and minimize the negatives, and it involves calling a truce of sorts between these two battling factions.

Failure may never be a close, personal friend—and we probably don't want it to be either—but failure *can* be a "frenemy." For better or worse, "frenemies" keep us on our game, and the "do I love you or do I hate you?" tension can be one of the most potent forces for change, and eventually success.

Another key, according to psychologist Michael Gervais, is to stay neutral. Neutral thinking doesn't mean you don't care about an outcome; it just means that you don't swing wildly between toxic positivity and catastrophizing. Staying neutral is really just about being as objective as possible when things go wrong. Easier said than done, of course, but like everything else in this book, practice goes a long way to making it possible.

And finally, don't let your self-worth get tied up in outcomes, says Jamie Kern Lima, entrepreneur and founder of IT cosmetics. Your idea may have failed, it might hurt, but *you* as a human are not a failure. The pain of failure and the awareness that it's necessary for progress must coexist, and though we may never achieve perfect balance between them, it is possible to keep the peace between these two realities as long as when you do fail, you gather data, make adjustments, and then keep moving forward.

So how do you know when you have an unhealthy relationship with failure? Consider the "MVP." If you've worked in or around tech, or specifically as a software engineer, then you know that the concept of the minimum viable product is the bare-bones version of your offering—something you launch after a sprint, perhaps in a weekend. It's always incomplete, and it's usually not very visually sophisticated, and if there are words involved, a few are likely misspelled. The goal is to move fast, get a "V 1.0" out there in the market. *Who cares?* everyone thinks. *We launched. We put something out in the world. We're gonna get some "data." We're winning. And now it's our job to make it better. Great job, everybody!*

This idea is mostly ~~horseshit~~ misunderstood. And let me tell you why.

Too often people interpret this to mean "make garbage," but that's not what this means. If you put garbage out in the world, and it fails, does that really give you meaningful data? It does not. Earlier in this book, we talked about paying attention to what was working, but if you put out a near-worthless first try and none of it works at all, of what value is that other than a waste of time and attention? The goal here is to find a balance between speed and quality, and—like most things—the only way to find that balance is by repeating the process of putting out drafts, or MVPs, in many areas of your life.

The key to meaningful failure is that you've first got *to make a real effort and be invested emotionally* before you can honestly fail. Trying is risky, caring is risky, and doing the best you can and then failing anyway hurts. But it's good to be disappointed when something doesn't go your way—whether it's a business decision, a relationship, or falling short of another goal you've worked toward. It means you cared enough in the first place for a failure to wake you up to possibility and maybe even point you in a new direction.

Everything Is an Experiment

From an early age, we're taught to pay attention to the high-lights of other people's lives, to lionize the accomplishments of pro athletes and legendary artists without understanding how much they had to fail to get where they are. But occasionally you get a glimpse of the truth.

In a tearful speech after winning a 2024 Grammy for best R&B song, which Lizzo presented, SZA said, "Lizzo and I have been friends since 2013, when we were both on a tiny Red Bull tour together opening up in small rooms for like 100 people, and to be on this stage with her is so amazing, I'm so grateful. . . . I came really, really far, and I can't believe this is happening." A triumphant moment, sure, but more importantly, one that showed something of the time, hard work, sacrifice, and the many struggles that it took to get there.

That's why all failure is *not* equal.

There are three types of failure, according to Dr. Amy Edmondson, author and award-winning professor at Harvard Business School. Before you move forward—and if you're tired of playing it so safe—it's wise to be aware of which kind of failure you're dealing with, so you can better learn from your mistakes.

Basic Failure

A basic failure looks like this: you did a thing, and it didn't work because you overlooked some basic protocols or best prac-tices. This kind of failure is simple cause-and-effect and, in the grand scheme of learning, it's the least useful because the reason it occurs is so straightforward. As long as you don't do that thing again, and you can reasonably adapt what you learned to that and other similar situations, problem solved.

Take, for example, the 2004 Super Bowl halftime show. Pop icon Janet Jackson experienced a wardrobe malfunction that exposed her breast on live television. The incident, later dubbed "Nipplegate," led to surprise and laughter in some circles but widespread outrage in others. Ultimately, some serious fines were imposed on broadcasters by the Federal Communications Commission (FCC). The failure in this case was preventable through wardrobe planning and rehearsal protocols, highlighting the need for a higher level of preparation for ultrahigh-profile live performances. Boobs on display, but not a lot to learn.

Complex Failure

Complex failures have multiple causes and occur in highly dynamic environments, so they're difficult to understand or remedy. Medical mistakes fit this definition as do battlefield errors and supply chain issues. When you're dealing with a lot of inputs, it's not easy to pinpoint the cause of a complex failure because of the many layers of uncertainty and interdependencies. These are the hardest failures to learn from because of just how messy they can be.

During the 1980 Winter Olympics in Lake Placid, New York, the far superior and heavily favored Soviet Union lost to the underdog United States men's ice hockey team in a stunning upset. The victory, known in the U.S. media as the "Miracle on Ice," captivated the United States and was a triumph of teamwork, perseverance, and national pride—but it was also seen as a massive failure from the Soviet perspective. The complex nature of such a failure, however, lay in the intricate dynamics of athletic competition, international politics, and cultural significance. Very difficult to unravel.

Intelligent Failure

In Edmondson's framework, an intelligent failure occurs when experimentation and risk-taking lead to valuable learning and innovation, despite initial setbacks. It is the preferred kind of failure because it is the variety that is most closely associated with the clearest path to growth and innovation.

Successful entrepreneurs have historically reveled in this type of failure, and Orville and Wilbur Wright were no exception. In their pursuit of powered flight, the brothers faced numerous setbacks and failures as they experimented with different aircraft designs and propulsion systems. Despite initial struggles and crashes, the Wright brothers persisted in their efforts, applying lessons learned from each failure to refine their approach. Their perseverance ultimately culminated in the first successful powered flight in 1903, marking a pivotal moment in aviation history.

We can't always control which kind of failure we face, but we can treat our own lives like an ongoing science project and aim to engineer the conditions that support us bringing more intelligent failures into existence. As a creative person, it often helps to imagine your life as a laboratory where you are the chief scientist running experiments all day long, every day. You start with a theory, mix a few ideas together to see what happens, then document the process, analyze the results, and build on those findings. As confidence and trust in your abilities and your systems grow, so do your desire, comfort, and wisdom to take risks at the right times. When we improve at the fine art of running such experiments, we get better at failing—and in turn we become better at living.

Get Good at Failing Well

At first, it's frightening to think of taking responsibility for all this failure you'll encounter once you truly start living. To that end, here are some thoughts on learning to fail well.

Full Benefit and Radical Ownership

Jocko Willink, the Navy SEAL turned author, is one of the most well-known thought leaders in the world, but the story behind the idea that made him famous is one of terrible heartbreak.

In the TED Talk that inspired his book, *Extreme Ownership*, Jocko shares the painful details of a military operation gone awry. While deployed in Iraq, Jocko's unit opened fire on another group only to discover when the "fog of war" lifted that they'd just killed one of their own men and wounded three more. As the leader of one of the units, Jocko was responsible for reporting back to his commander about what had happened. As he reviewed every mistake and the men involved, he saw plenty of blame to go around, and it was tempting to point the finger at other people. But by the time he began to debrief his commanding officers, he had come to an inevitable conclusion about who was ultimately responsible.

"It was my fault," he told his supervisor.

Instead of getting fired or losing credibility with his men, Jocko found that his unit ultimately respected him more. His commander trusted him more. And the millions who heard his speech were moved by his story, quoting him in countless articles and speeches afterward as an example of someone who stepped forward to take responsibility rather than shying away from it.

"When a team takes ownership of its problems," he says in his TED Talk, "the problems get solved."

This is true in all areas of life: on the battlefield, in creativity, in business, and in every interaction we have with others. And it's only by accepting our own role in failures that we can receive the full benefit of what each failure has to offer.

It turns out that the "full benefit" offers a lot. According to business leader Paul Marobella (from whom I first heard the term), *full benefit* is actually a term used by the U.S. Navy SEALs to describe the upside of any situation that's gone completely wrong. "It is more than just a phrase," says Marobella. "It's a mindset that encourages one to squeeze every ounce of value from every situation. The highs, lows, and in-between hold a lesson, an opportunity for growth and learning."

When you look at it that way, "extreme ownership" becomes the obvious path through the wilderness of failure because it's the only reliable way to fully see a situation, own the results, good or bad, and then evolve from there. The steps are clear: first, we accept radical responsibility for everything that has happened to us, especially the embarrassing and unfortunate parts; then we debrief and figure out what went wrong. Finally—and only from here—we can courageously commit to learning as much as we possibly can from those experiences. Again, we are the artists and scientists of our own experience, and failure is the data we must use to build a creative life we love. Anything else is pretend. There is no other way.

Rejection Therapy

So what keeps us from experimenting, failing, owning our failures, reaping the full benefit, and then trying again?

It's not failure itself. It's fear of failure.

Years ago, I gave a keynote at the World Domination Summit in Portland, Oregon, a spectacular conference created and run for a decade by the author and entrepreneur Chris Guillebeau. Unfortunately for me, my talk followed Jia Jiang's. This was the first time he had given this particular speech on a large stage—and it would go on to become legendary. His story is a special one that I share "on blast" whenever and wherever I can because it's a fantastic example of how to navigate fear and cultivate resilience.

Jia emigrated from China to the United States as a cultural exchange student to pursue his teenage dream of building the biggest company in the world and buying Microsoft. Fast-forward fifteen years. He was thirty years old, married, expecting a baby, and working in corporate America. He hadn't bought Microsoft. "It felt so shiny on the outside," he said, "but so wrong on the inside."

When Jia looked at his life, all he could see was that he had chosen security over his dream of entrepreneurship. So at the behest of his wife, he quit his job just days before his baby was born and gave himself six months to work on building his company from scratch. Pursuing his dream involved rejection after rejection, and even though Jia *thought* he was resilient, each time he failed to secure funding or hire the right employee, it hurt. He finally realized that even though he had been conventionally successful, it was partially because he had spent a lifetime running away from failure. In the process, he had rejected himself, his intuition, and his desire to build a different kind of life.

One night, while searching online for how to get comfortable with rejection, Jia found Canadian entrepreneur Jason Comely's idea of Rejection Therapy, which is the practice of exposing yourself to rejection to desensitize yourself to the experience of failure so that you can become more resilient.

While at first he was skeptical and fearful of the experiment, he quickly came to love it, and set himself the challenge of seeking rejection every day for one hundred days straight. He asked for $100 from the security guard at his workplace, he asked a police officer if he could drive his cop car, and he asked his local Krispy Kreme shop to fashion him a custom donut in the style of Olympic rings. While the security guard didn't give him the money, the cop let him take his car for a spin, and Jackie, the Krispy Kreme manager, did in fact fulfill his request for the five-ring Olympic logo from donuts—for free. Someone else let him play soccer in their backyard, and another man let him fly his tiny plane.

As Jia went on, he realized that even the nos were far more nuanced than he had realized when he was spending all his time and energy avoiding them. When someone said no, they often invited him to explain why he was asking his question and created an opening for him to refine his ask and receive a yes. Or one man said he didn't want Jia to plant flowers in his backyard, but then explained it wasn't because he didn't like flowers but rather because his dog would dig them up. Then he sent Jia across the street to plant the flowers in a neighbor's yard. At the end of one hundred days, Jia learned that the world is a kinder, more welcoming place than he previously believed.

But he also learned that most rejection isn't personal, the same way that most failures say little about who you are as a person. Ideas fail, experiments fail, relationships fail, even our bodies fail. But in none of these cases does it make *you* a failure, and it doesn't make *you* unworthy of success. The sooner we can detach our identities from our failures, the sooner we can internalize the idea that we are worthy of success, the better off we'll be. And as Jia learned, if we are willing to consider what *seems* impossible and get comfortable with asking for help, we will quite often be pleasantly surprised.

Consider taking on a bit of Rejection Therapy as a tiny experiment of your own. Any version of asking and hearing no's will work, but if you want to build this muscle quickly, try making your first few asks so absurd that you are nearly certain you'll get shut down. Ask your server for a free bottle of Dom Perignon if you agree to order the rib eye, ask the forklift operator at Costco if she can lift up your car out in the parking lot so you can quickly change the oil, or ask the zookeeper if it might be possible to take a little swim with the penguins. The point here is to desensitize yourself to "failing" and empower yourself to take chances with less of the fear that far too often holds us back.

Avoiding the Failure Trap

Ed Catmull, the visionary cofounder of Pixar, once famously declared, "Failure isn't a necessary evil—it's a necessary consequence of doing something new." And yet, in the uber-competitive creative industry, where original ideas are the hallmark of greatness and innovation is celebrated as a badge of honor, there lurks a quicksand for your dreams that I like to call the "Failure Trap." Ultimately, so many aspiring creatives—especially those early in their careers—fall victim to the seductive allure of playing it safe.

The insidious nature of the Failure Trap lies in its ability to disguise itself as prudence. It whispers sweet assurances of comfort and stability, tempting us to trade breakthroughs for safety and stability—which, you know from wherever you're reading this right now, is all an illusion anyway.

I know so many people—Carrie from San Bernardino, Bennett from Austin, and Amira from London for example—who have all at one time or another shared promises with me that they'll take more risks, "Later, when I have more [fill in the blank]"— experience, resources, time, money, etc., you name it. But it's no surprise that this elusive "someday" never arrives. As years pass and careers progress, the painful irony is that the stakes only seem to grow higher. Even modest success breeds complacency, and the fear of failure quickly becomes paralyzing. The very idea of risking what they have now—however modest or grand—for the chance to create something truly groundbreaking becomes increasingly terrifying. And so they settle, trapped in a cycle of incremental gains, disconnection, stagnation, and missed opportunities.

Gasp. Does this sound like you?

Here's the harsh truth: the cost of trying to avoid failure is far greater than the sting of failing—*if* you learn to fail well. By playing it safe, and clinging to the comfort of familiarity, you are risking your unlimited upside and your potential for greatness.

As such, I offer you a caution to avoid at all costs becoming a prisoner of your own fears, trapped in a cage of your own making. If you happen to find yourself paralyzed by the fear of falling short, remember this: the biggest risk you can take is not taking any risks at all. Embracing failure not as a foe to be feared, but as a faithful companion to know so well is the only path to the special sauce, the freedom, and the life you seek.

The Subjectivity of Failure

Once in 2010, a good while into my own personal entrepreneurial journey, I took a hard run at launching a startup that I believed really had the potential for a massive, positive impact. Over the years, I'd had a number of big ideas, but this was one I thought that could truly stick. And so, that year, my business partner at the time, Craig, and I started CreativeLive. At the time it was a completely revolutionary way of delivering online creative education. World-class instructors—think Grammy, Oscar, Emmy, and Pulitzer-winning artists; or iconic, game-changing entrepreneurs—delivering their wisdom live on the internet with a simple business model: anyone in the world could watch for free while we streamed the course live, but if you wanted to watch it again at any point in the future, you had to purchase the course.

Ambitious, for sure, and a bit uncanny—but we nailed it.

Right out of the gate, we regularly had 100,000 people from around the world watching live classes and the conversion rates for our customers from free-to-paid were orders of magnitude above any e-commerce industry standard. By the end of 2011, we knew we were both *serving* and *making* millions—and we'd come to realize that we had a tiger by the tail.

As with most things in life, it's rare to fully understand the nuances of a new opportunity. The excitement of growing a potential billion-dollar company was intoxicating. Venture capital firms caught wind of what we were doing and flocked to us in droves. In an effort to gain our favor and share in the upside of such an adventure, they told us our little company could be gigantic and transformative for the world. We shared their beliefs and, after adjudicating several offers, we bought into the money they were selling. Without going into the minutiae of VC funding models, it's fair to say we drank the Kool-Aid—and it wasn't for lack of thought or planning. We eventually raised significant capital—north of $50 million—without selling off the whole company; and with that money, we grew, we served more customers, expanded our offerings, and raised even more capital, which, in turn, brought even more people to the decision-making table.

The goal of venture capital is to grow a company as fast as you can, at all costs. By design, you end up spending more than you are earning in any given month just to keep the machine going—and that's just what we did. In our case, at one phase of the journey, we were burning an additional million dollars of cash each month above and beyond the millions we were making.

When I say grow at all costs, this is an example of what I mean.

The whole experience started to feel like an exercise in alternatively splashing violently out to sea toward some foggy goal only to be slurped back to shore by the undertow. *Spend, spend, spend. Grow, grow, grow.* And we still couldn't keep up with the expectations of our investors as they hungered for more growth and compared us to Twitter, Uber, and the other startups du jour. Not to make them out as the "bad guys" (most were men), but it's hard to overstate the size of their expectations relative to their dainty fleece vests. I was constantly working—leaving my family in Seattle to travel to San Francisco, New York, London, and other places to make sure everything was running as smoothly as possible, splitting my time between multiple homes, while never feeling at home in any of them.

At one point during this mission, I had to interrupt my role as founder and chairman to add the CEO title and responsibilities to my docket after the CEO I had hired to run the company just a couple years earlier was no longer able to keep up and lost the appreciation for the work. Revenues had flattened, operations were fluttering, and the culture of the company, once vibrant and booming, had become stale. I was nervous about the time it would take and potential risk involved in hiring another executive from outside the company, so I grabbed the reins.

It took some time. We had to transition dozens of employees who weren't right for the next phase of the journey out of the company and replace them with fresh, newly energized talent. We restructured our finances and almost entirely rebuilt operations from the ground up. Eventually, through the hard work of hundreds of people, we regained our mojo. I was proud of the team and of my leadership through the mess. By the end of 2017, we were doing $24 million on a $36 million "annual revenue run rate" (your most recent month's revenue multiplied by twelve, which signals your company's trajectory), and growing 40 percent yearly over the previous year. It felt incredible to have rebuilt the company, to be serving a revitalized and quickly growing customer base, and to be back on track for the imminent success we had imagined.

Or so I thought.

One day, after an all-company meeting where we'd just shared the latest great news about our direction up and to the right, I joined one of our investors in a conference room and told him I thought it was the perfect time to raise our next round of capital. We had dug ourselves out of a huge hole, and after several hard years, everything was growing again. The timing felt right, and I was certain he was going to tell me I was doing a great job.

"You know, Chase," he said with a sigh, "frankly, the business is just not that interesting."

All my life, I've prided myself on being someone who doesn't know how to lose. Give me a game, and I'll find a way to win. I did this with sports, and I did it with school. Hell, I even did it with my first career, having rather dramatically ascended the professional photography ranks as a young gun. I've always been scrappy as hell and good at figuring out how to get shit done. My experience with startup culture, however, was a bizarre and humbling one. I thought we were winning and was stunned to discover that this investor thought just the opposite. My, what a fickle beast is the market.

I was in the process of trying to build the best, most impactful version of CreativeLive while my business partners' primary interest was maximum scale, at timely intervals, in order to facilitate their own financially engineered business model that I was just learning to understand.

I remember the shock and disbelief walking out of that conference room. Our investor was quiet. Neither of us felt like winners. We were looking at two sides of the same coin, and we knew we'd need to find alignment at some point soon—and it would have to be a compromise between our respective visions of the future.

It's not uncommon for this to be true in entrepreneurship or even when several people witness a crime. Any detective or lawyer will tell you that eyewitness testimony varies greatly from one witness to another, despite them experiencing the exact same event. From my perspective, we were on a newly minted rocket ship: we were revitalized, expanding our offerings to the community, and everything looked exactly like what we'd drawn up on the whiteboard prior to me taking over the CEO role.

But from the perspective of a venture capitalist who wants to see a company go to a billion dollars or to zero as quickly as possible, it was a difficult place to be. It's the equivalent of the "friend zone" in dating: too nice to bail, not special enough to go all in. This is the sad truth about startup culture. We often hear that something like 75 percent of VC-funded startups fail. But the reality is they don't fail at being good businesses—after all, ours would go on to serve tens of millions of students, make hundreds of millions of dollars, and be acquired by a large, publicly traded company. But where we failed was at being the next Instagram or Amazon. That's mostly all that matters to a certain kind of investor. There just weren't enough digits in our growth percentage or our revenue lines to steal the hearts of a very narrow set of capitalists who shape the market.

Ventures like ours are specifically funded to scale massively, and when a company doesn't align with those incredibly high expectations, it's called a *failure*. As a result, these companies are often ignored, minimized, shut down, or driven into obscurity. In our case, though, we didn't see it as a failure. Lots of us who built the company learned that things can look one way from the sidelines and completely different on the field.

It was in a follow-up to that investor meeting that I did some real soul-searching and decided to focus the company on winning the game we wanted to play instead of losing the one others expected us to play.

In life, you and I are not responsible for other people's scorecards. That's not something we can control. We are responsible for the standards we hold ourselves to and how we define "success." That's what Jocko Willink means by "extreme ownership." If what we want is misaligned with reality, or not in step with those we are partnering with, then we either need to refocus our efforts or change the tune. I've had these moments more than a few times in life, and they always teach me something. Put simply, I feel strongly that I have received the "full benefit" of such failures.

What about you? Have you grown tired of playing it safe? Have you, like me, learned that you cannot compromise your responsibility to yourself? It's a painful but very valuable lesson.

When I was trying to please my investors, growing a company in which they'd hedged their beliefs, it was killing my health, hurting my family, and making it difficult to keep my hopes and dreams alive. But when I finally reassessed my situation, isolated the variables that were accounting for my unhappiness, and made some changes in what I could control—everything else changed too.

Sometimes, what one person calls a "meh" is really just another kind of success. When you find yourself in such a situation, the hard part is to let go of what others may think and do what's best for your most authentic self and those around you in your care. One person's success is another person's failure. It all comes down to what game you're playing. The wisdom comes in realizing that this is entirely up to you.

Reframing Failure

In her groundbreaking work, Carol Dweck famously distinguished between fixed mindset and growth mindset. Those who adopt a fixed mindset tend to see themselves as the kind of people whose positive or negative attributes are immutable and prevent them from making any sort of change. Every failure is a confirmation that their instincts are poor, and they will never improve. Those who adopt a growth mindset, by contrast, see setbacks as a lesson. They can learn from mistakes and failure. Their achievements aren't only a result of natural abilities; they can affect the future through effort and determination.

There's a scene in the hit show *Ted Lasso* that illustrates this. The eponymous main character coaches one of his players who keeps beating himself up for his mistakes. Coach Lasso tells Sam that a goldfish is the happiest animal on earth. Why? Because it only has a ten-second memory. "Be a goldfish," he tells Sam. That's good advice for us all when it comes to dealing with the initial sting of failure and then picking ourselves up and moving on.

Early in his career, LeVar Burton had the good fortune of being cast as Kunta Kinte in the smash hit miniseries *Roots*, based on the bestselling novel by Alex Haley. This opened a lot of doors for him, but by the early 1980s, the phone stopped ringing. And LeVar wasn't prepared to deal with the rejection.

Having been an overnight success for a few shining moments, he wondered why he should even *have* to audition. After all, he'd just been part of a groundbreaking miniseries. But after a few failed auditions, he realized he'd need to change his approach if he ever wanted to act again. So he took a good hard look in the mirror and accepted the fact that his attitude wasn't helping.

"I was killing myself before I was really fully in the room," LeVar told me. Success had made him complacent, and he had begun to see himself as someone who didn't have to try anymore to make his dreams come true.

Nothing clarifies like failure, though. After a number of rejections, he decided to reframe these experiences. It wasn't that he, an already famous and successful actor, *had* to audition. This was something he *got* to do. It was an opportunity, not an obligation. These auditions were not beneath him. They were the bridge he needed to continue doing what he loved.

With this simple reframe, things slowly turned around for LeVar. He started getting callbacks and was eventually cast in new roles. His second career began, leading to memorable roles in *Reading Rainbow*, *Star Trek: The Next Generation*, and many other creative endeavors. Had he never learned the crucial lesson from his failures, we would likely have never seen more of his artistry, his philanthropic work, or his social justice advocacy.

Success is, of course, fun. But we have to remember that we aren't our successes—any more than we are our failures. They are just things that happen to us. We have to keep doing the work, moving through the challenges presented at each and every turn of our journey. When we stop failing, we stop learning. And when we stop learning, we stop growing.

"We need to be brutally honest with ourselves," LeVar said to me. If you want to win, you have to ask yourself the tough questions and be willing to hear the hard answers. It was when he looked honestly within himself that he started to grow again. People noticed a shift in his attitude, and how he was showing up to auditions began to look different. That changed everything.

This is leverage too: getting out of a life where you're stuck and into a life that shines a light on the areas where you want to improve. Once the lever of failure starts moving and we become more aware, it can push us in the direction of growth and transformation. Like anything, this requires inner work, but it's worth it. The juice is worth the squeeze.

Five Rules for Failing

The ability to turn our failures into successes is an art form, one that must be mastered. This takes time and a healthy dose of patience, but there are also a handful of important mindset shifts—aka "rules for failing"—that can accelerate learning across nearly any discipline.

Rule #1: Don't Fail Before You Fail

Imagine you have a great idea, but before you even think about sharing it with other people or trying to make something of it, you shut yourself down. *I don't have time. I'm not the right person. Maybe it's not such a great idea after all. Who am I to think I could pull this off?* Two or three years down the road, someone builds *exactly* that company, opens *exactly* that store, or writes *exactly* that book, and you're kicking yourself.

You can broadly apply this viewpoint to so many things in life. How many times have you quit before you've even really started?

So next time, before you veto yourself, stay home and play it safe, ignore your instincts and intuition, and reject your own best ideas, think again. The world will put plenty of obstacles in the way of achieving your dreams; there's no reason to do it yourself.

Rule #2: Don't Fail to Suck

You decide you want to snowboard, so you head to the bunny hill, catch an edge, and get slammed into the packed snow. What did you expect? Flying through the backcountry, carving lines through powder, and a beautiful, video-worthy ride?

Unlikely, my friend. Even for the most coordinated and confident among us, it's rare to be good at something new right away; it's far more likely that we'll be mediocre or even terrible. So the rule here is to embrace the suck! Be willing to struggle, look funny, and make mistakes because nobody finds proficiency, let alone becomes a master, without months, even years, of practice. We all need to see failing as a necessary part of learning and treat being unskilled at something as either worthy of a laugh or as a badge of honor.

Rule #3: Fail—a Lot

Tiger Woods, largely considered the best to ever play the game of golf, misses the green from just a hundred yards away 20 percent of the time. He's got GOAT status and he *still* fails to complete a task that nearly every golfer thinks they ought to be able to do—an amazing one out of five times. Whenever I am out golfing with my buddies and bring this fact up, they usually don't believe me. I ordinarily have to wait for them to take out their phones and find this factoid before they'll capitulate. After that, they lighten up (and the irony is that they tend to play better once the pressure is off).

But then it begs the question: How many greens has Tiger *ever tried to hit* in his life of practice and professional play in order to have the distinct honor to only find success in four out of five tries? The answer? A gazillion! A professional of Tiger's quality—or anything close to that, really—has likely attempted this feat more in each year than the average or better golfer will attempt in a lifetime! The repetition at that caliber of play is unreal.

With this in mind, it ought to become okay to be 106 yards out and miss the green. Failure is a part of the game, even for the best in the world. Your primary goal then should become to get in as many reps as you can to close in on the next level available to you.

Rule #4: Fail Fast

You don't just want to fail. You want to fail forward, with some sort of intention about how you can use this to grow and get better. This is a key vector in Amy Edmondson's research, and I agree. Inertia from successive failures is a key attribute of not just success and triumph, but fulfillment as well. There's also a rich understanding that develops through increasingly smaller windows between attempts, and failing fast also creates a sense of fulfillment through learning and momentum through doing.

"Keep going," as author and artist Austin Kleon would say.

The best way to do this is to run lots of tiny experiments that don't threaten your daily livelihood, and then scale up from there. Remember that momentum is mo-betta. The possibility of failing should rarely be a do-or-die scenario—if ever. And when it is, let's hope you've taken some time and practice to work up to those superhigh stakes.

Rule #5: Fail Publicly

At the start of the chapter, I talked about the fact that everyone is failing all the time even though we rarely see it. Or if we eventually do, it's just a few minor failures embedded in the highlight reel to show how spectacular someone's success is later on. Brené Brown calls this "gold-plated grit," when we tell a story and pretend to be vulnerable, but we really just gloss over the tough bits so we can seem empathetic and connected before rushing back to looking good.

Let's stop all that BS and start normalizing struggle, trial, failure, and beyond. It's fine to fail in private, but the stakes tend to be too low. Get comfortable with being uncomfortable. Talk about when something goes wrong in your newsletter, in a blog post, over coffee, or on a podcast. You'll be surprised at how many people will come out of the woodwork to share their own stories of setbacks, and in the process you may get some connection, help, or valuable advice.

Never Fail to Try

We're all programmed to think mistakes are bad, and perfection is good. But life is not about avoiding mistakes—we all make them, and we always will. It's about recovering from them a little bit more quickly every time. When you do that, self-trust, confidence, and intuition will follow, all of which we need as adults and for a lifetime. We may never love failure, but we *can* get a little better each time at tolerating it and maybe peacefully coexisting.

While failure is one of our best teachers, it also has an equally important purpose—it builds resilience. Sadly, we cannot build resilience on the back of win after win. It takes difficulty, challenge, obstacles, and rejection to show us what we are truly capable of.

If you don't fail, you end up living a seemingly safe but small life. If you want a bigger life, one filled with adventure and surprise, you'll eventually have to take some bigger risks. Don't wait to get started—small failures often lead to small successes. And big failures, when you're ready for them and if you can recover from them, lead to even bigger successes.

I'm willing to bet that taking risks and building the resilience it will take to not play it safe is one of the main reasons you're reading this book. The old you wouldn't have picked it up—the new you knows that failure is a prerequisite for freedom; that adversity is a prerequisite to growth; that creativity is a prerequisite for building a life you love, which all lie beyond playing it safe.

Lever 7

Practice

Success Leaves Clues

It's often puzzling for us mere mortals to watch the best in the world practice their crafts—whatever those crafts might be. We stare in amazement and wonder what it might be like to be so gifted, at anything really.

Lucky for us, success leaves clues.

In the world of basketball, few shine as brightly as Stephen Curry, affectionately known as "Steph." Curry was born and raised in Akron, Ohio, and his journey to basketball stardom is as remarkable as it is inspiring. Despite coming from a family deeply rooted in basketball—his father, Dell Curry, was a professional NBA player—Steph's path to greatness was anything but guaranteed. But today, Steph Curry is widely regarded as one of the greatest shooters of all time. He holds several NBA championship titles, numerous NBA records, multiple MVP awards, and is the unequivocal best three-point shooter of all time.

Standing at a modest six feet three inches tall, Curry didn't fit the typical mold of a basketball superstar. Yet, what he lacks in height, he more than makes up for in determination and an unparalleled work ethic. From a young age, Curry displayed an innate talent for shooting the basketball, beginning his long journey of honing his craft in his family's backyard. But what truly sets Curry apart is not just his natural gift for the sport, or even his humility and grace outside the game. His coaches and peers are quick to point to his relentless dedication to practice and improvement that sets Curry apart from all the rest. And it's not just about his commitment to logging hours on the court, coming early, or staying late after practice either. You can see an unmistakable difference just watching him practice (go ahead—check him out on YouTube). Seeing him shoot the ball reveals a seemingly insane sense of precision and intentionality that few others can match.

Just as Steph Curry is not your average hoops star, Yasmeen Lari is not your average architect. Born in Pakistan in 1941, Lari defied societal expectations and charted a path that has made her one of the most fascinating figures in modern architecture. Her journey to architectural prominence—and specifically the core attributes of her practice—is as unconventional as it is motivating.

Through her pioneering work with the Heritage Foundation of Pakistan, Lari has spearheaded efforts to usher Pakistan's rich architectural heritage into contemporary times. In a field dominated by profit margins, big buildings, and even bigger egos, she has made her mark through rehabilitating historic buildings, revitalizing urban neighborhoods, and empowering marginalized communities. You might expect the most lavish projects and eye-catching designs to separate one architect from another—or in this case the outputs from her studio in the city of Lahore from the studios and firms of her peers. But that isn't the case here. Stunning and sharp as her designs might be, what is most noteworthy about her practice is not just the quality of the output, but rather the role that the *input* plays in her work.

You see, Lari starts each day with a morning walk through the historic streets of Lahore, and not purely for exercise. She doesn't meditate on architecture or sketch the next big thing. She mingles with residents from the neighborhoods where future projects are brewing in her head. Of course she is drawing inspiration from the city's rich architectural heritage, but what is more remarkable about her practice is the nature and quality of the time she spends with the city's *people*, fostering dialogue and connecting with locals at heritage sites to better hone her sensibilities for her preservation and restoration efforts, which blend traditional craftsmanship with modern techniques.

Joshua Roman is a name synonymous with excellence in the world of classical music. Born in Oklahoma City, Oklahoma, in 1983, Roman showed a natural aptitude for the cello at a young age. His talent was evident early on, and he quickly rose through the ranks to become one of the most respected and sought-after cellists of his generation. Yo-Yo Ma called Roman "one of the great exemplars of the 21st century musician."

It's not just Roman's talent, his innovative interpretations, or his fearless approach to performance that set him apart. What truly distinguishes Roman is his approach to practice. While all top cellists devote countless hours to honing their craft, Roman takes a more holistic approach, incorporating mindfulness and exercise alongside his daily practice of getting better at practice itself. But that's not where he stops. One time, while recording a video of himself preparing for a solo performance in Seattle where he would debut the song "Hallelujah" by Leonard Cohen (including his own vocals alongside the rich and ever-so-warm sound of his multi-million dollar, centuries-old Stradivarius), Joshua shared with me that he was also in the process of a new kind of practicing. "Every day for the past year-plus, I've practiced a different one of the Unaccompanied Solo Bach Cello Suites."

For the benefit of the layperson, this particular collection of compositions is arguably *the* defining collection of music that highlights the technical range, universality, and emotional depth of the cello, not to mention that the unaccompanied solo cellist is tasked with playing multiple melodic lines simultaneously, creating the illusion of harmony and counterpoint. It's been the bedrock of the cello repertoire for more than three hundred years and contains the most technically demanding pieces of music ever written for this instrument. And Joshua has been practicing this masterwork *every single day*—for years on end.

In a word, the attention required of Joshua for that level of practice is profound.

Considering these masters, it would be easy to register the sheer volume of time and repetition required of top performers like Curry, Lari, and Roman—and call it good. And you'd be right, on one account. It's easy to see what sets each of them apart from others in their respective fields. But with even a little bit of excavating, one quickly begins to see striking similarities that connect them to one another and to other masters from time immemorial. There is a pattern in how they practice that each and every one of us can adopt. And it's based on three pillars I describe below.

The Three Pillars of Practice

The Fundamentals

Roman, Curry, and Lari each focus ruthlessly on the basics of their craft with shocking precision. Of course, they have unimaginable fringe skills that run across every aspect of their repertoire as well, but what they disproportionately practice, ad infinitum, are the fundamentals.

For Joshua, it's nailing every note that the cello can play, then pairing those notes with every conceivable note around them to create a near-infinite set of configurations. Every day, he's exploring the full range of the instrument, discovering and rediscovering its possibilities.

For Yasmeen, it's focusing not on the radical design du jour but rather on the radical notion that architecture is meant to serve people and change lives. By concentrating her practice on understanding the hopes, dreams, and desires of the people she serves, she is inextricably attuned to the purpose of the profession to which she has dedicated her life.

For Steph, he approaches each practice session with a clear

sense of purpose and intentionality. Whether he's working on his shooting technique, ball-handling skills, or footwork, every rep is aligned with specific game situations, rather than abstract concepts, and is executed with precision and focus. "He wipes the slate clean after every shot and always believes his next shot is going in," Alan Stein Jr., one of Curry's former coaches, told me when speaking about the hoops legend. He pays meticulous attention to detail, constantly seeking ways to refine and improve not just the outcomes of his practice, but his very practice itself.

In this regard, the best in the world don't actually have any special tricks that you or I don't have. They are simply focusing on the fundamentals that everyone knows are important, but which most of us lack the discipline to practice day in and day out.

The Process

Each of them has fallen in love with the *process* of practicing. Practicing is a joy. Sure, Curry might love the tension of a playoff game, Roman the electricity of a performance at Carnegie Hall, or Lari the ribbon-cutting ceremony on a restored building going back into use, but without a doubt, they each demonstrate a passion for every type of practice: the skills, the discipline, and the mindset. It's through this raw passion for the craft itself that they are able—excited even—to work long hours and to build experience, from which comes trust, proof, and confidence, in turn.

Philosopher Alan Watts remarked that the same is true

for any great artist: "If you are a great artist, your so called 'periods of practice'—when you, say, sit for hours and study your technique on the piano—you will not do that effectively unless it is a pleasure for you. You have to come to the point that going over it again and again is a dance."

The same can be said for entrepreneurs like Gary Vaynerchuk. Gary has told me many times, both behind closed doors and out loud in public, that he loves the spirit of entrepreneurship so much that it's no longer only about winning. "I've even learned to love an L [slang for loss] now and then," he said to me once as we took the stage together for a speaking gig in New York. "That's how much I love the game [of business]."

As the saying goes, the person who loves walking will walk further than the person who loves the destination.

The Identity

Arguably the most important thing we can learn from studying how the world's top performers practice in almost any discipline is that they all have aligned how they practice with who they are. This is a powerful insight because it is the most broadly applicable—for you, me, and anyone who wants to come along. They identify themselves in a particular way; say, for example, as someone who wants greatness—aka someone who is great and expects greatness—with how they show up in the world. Thoughts, beliefs, actions, it's all aligned.

Why? Because identity, it turns out, is an incredibly powerful alignment tool for shaping habits in humans. If you think of yourself as on a diet, you are less likely to eat as clean than if you think of yourself as "a healthy person." By contrast, if you think of yourself as a "smoker who is trying to quit" instead of a healthy person who has discarded old habits that no longer serve you, you actually still identify as "a smoker" and are less likely to be able to quit. Essentially, we are wired for language and the way we speak about ourselves and think about ourselves—how we *honestly identify in our heart and mind*—is one of the most effective and important psychological mechanisms known to drive behavior.

It's actually a pretty straightforward psychological framework. There was a time long ago when Steph Curry, Yasmeen Lari, and Joshua Roman all pictured a future version of themselves: world-class at their respective crafts. It was this picture—this set of attributes and behaviors they would need to embody—that helped them reverse engineer how they would show up in the world. They first began to speak and think about themselves in a new way, and then they behaved and ultimately *practiced* like the person they saw in their mind's eye.

Simple but not easy.

To translate this into more practical terms, consider, if you will, a future self, a future version of you. If you could snap your fingers and be living that dream of yours, what would your life look like—thoughts and actions for starters—for that amazing future to be true?

Let's say, for example, that you want to be a Michelin-starred chef one day, so this is the future-self state that you want. You'd begin this exercise by deconstructing what a Michelin-star chef would think and then live and exemplify those traits. What kinds of friends would she have, where and how would she spend her time, what would she read and study? What actions would she take each day through that lens of existence? Essentially what would her *practice* look like?

Or in another case, if you want to run a sub-2:30 marathon, can you determine what that life would be like—what *you* would be like—if that were true? Or how about if you identified as a social entrepreneur whose goal is to feed free meals to a billion people? From any of those places, it would be easy to understand, or at least easy to build a set of beliefs, tools, and practices, for what your day, week, month, and year would look like. Or, lastly, if you think of yourself as someone who has the potential to reclaim your world and live a rich, creative, and bold life, then you'd probably, for starters, identify as someone who would most definitely be reading/have read *Never Play It Safe* several times. So there's a behavior, an action, a step, and a mindset to adopt right away.

At its essence, you can either allow an almost-random set of daily actions that the world has prescribed to create your identity, or you can put a stake in the ground and make room for your authentic self, embrace your core beliefs, and support your desired future self. Ultimately, this is about the freedom to choose. The more you identify and behave as if you already are your future self, the more clear your life's practices become. This is what the best in the world know about practice that the rest of the world does not. In the words of James Clear, author of *Atomic Habits*, the definitive book on changing behaviors that has spent hundreds of weeks atop the *New York Times* bestseller list: "Every action you take is a vote for the kind of person you want to become."

Principles of Practice x 10

Anders Ericsson was a Swedish psychologist renowned for his groundbreaking research on expertise and deliberate practice. His work has had a profound impact on fields ranging from sports and music to education and psychology. Ericsson and his colleagues conducted dozens of studies examining the factors that contribute to expert performance across various domains, including music, sports, chess, and medicine. They found that deliberate practice, rather than innate talent alone, played *the* crucial role in distinguishing expert performers from lesser performers.

Deliberate practice can be defined as any highly structured and effortful activity aimed at improving performance. It involves identifying specific goals, receiving feedback, and engaging in regular, focused, and disciplined sessions designed to enhance strengths and remedy weaknesses with the ultimate intention of pushing the boundaries of one's abilities.

One of the most famous concepts associated with this research is "the 10,000 hour rule," which was popularized by Malcolm Gladwell in his book *Outliers*. While Ericsson's work didn't specifically draw this conclusion—that it took some prescribed amount of time to achieve mastery (which has been scientifically discredited since then)—his work was at the center of this popular and well-reasoned idea that focused effort yields results. Hard to argue with that because it matches our own experiences.

But just as we have understood through deconstructing the practices and the lives of Roman, Curry, and Lari, Anders's research signaled that the concept of practice transcends just "putting in the time and logging the repetitions." Therefore, dear reader, I offer you the following list of ten principles that precipitate from the key attributes of practice that opened the chapter:

1. **Most people confuse complexity with quality.** Do not fall into this trap. The truth is just the opposite. Learn to direct your attention to the practices that embody the most fundamental aspects of anything you're trying to learn, be, or become. Most people will tell you that they thrive *despite* having simple practices when they are actually thriving *because* of simple practices.

2. **Practice is fleeting impermanence.** Whatever happened yesterday is gone. Whatever might happen in the future isn't real—it's an idea. You are not what you think, your only experience is what you do. All we have is now, so show up and practice the best version of yourself *today*.

3. **Practice flows from an innate desire within you.** Everything is practice. Your natural state is one of freedom and you possess the power to choose. You are in a constant state of learning and growing. You are biologically wired to simultaneously be able to enjoy the present moment and have a preference for the possibility of a different you. When you are not inspired to practice, know that this is normal. Psychological resistance is part of the game. As Steven Pressfield says, "Resistance is experienced as fear;

the degree of fear equates to the strength of Resistance. Therefore the more fear we feel about a specific enterprise, the more certain we can be that that enterprise is important to us and to the growth of our soul."

4. **Be passionate about everything you get a chance to practice.** Yes, I do mean everything, including the most difficult states, moments, and stages of our lives. Including the laundry. Including the difficult conversation. Trust that the universe is providing you with these opportunities to develop your practice.

5. **Practice is repetition.** "How we spend our days is, of course, how we spend our lives," wrote Annie Dillard. So practice is simultaneously the easiest thing in the world and the most difficult. It feels simple when we are able to repeat doing what we love over and over again until it becomes a habit. It feels difficult whenever we face resistance *or* when we perceive repetition as boring. Remember, boredom isn't about the *object* of our attention, but rather the lack of *quality* of the attention. Ultimately, we are what we practice, so choose carefully.

6. **Practice requires resistance.** The act of practicing, on some level, requires another type of resistance, different from the psychological resistance discussed above. In this case, resistance training is all about tension and opposition, just like building a muscle. The safe, tidy life you were taught to live is like a weight. It's like gravity pulling you down. So it should be no surprise that you must exert

effort to move. This is natural and should be trusted. Just like we must employ our muscles to overcome the earth pulling us toward its center, and we must use our intuition and intellect to overcome strategic problems. This is the only way we grow and get better at anything. Often, we think of challenges as obstacles to be overcome, but the fact is the difficulty of a task is what builds a skill in the first place. Consider the practice of getting stronger, for example. It's not lifting the same amount of weight that creates the muscle. Rather, it's increasing the weight once you reach a certain level of proficiency that causes the gains.

7. **Practice is about perseverance.** A natural consequence of practice is that you eventually become better at whatever it is you are practicing (and get better at the skill of practicing!). Gains stabilize. Proficiency sets in. By no means is this a bad thing, but it is a state of which we should be aware. Aikido master George Leonard calls this place of familiarity with a skill the "plateau." If you've ever learned an instrument or tried to improve your golf game, you've likely experienced it before. In fact, this is an important part of any practice. However, what we do with these seasons of stability determines how far we go in our own pursuit of mastery. In his book *Mastery*, Leonard writes, "If our life is a good one, a life of mastery, most of it will be spent on the plateau. If not, a large part of it may well be spent in restless, distracted, ultimately self-destructive attempts to escape the plateau." The goal of a master is to not always be improving. But it is to always be practicing.

8. **Practice requires prioritization.** We can't master everything. By definition, mastery is an exclusive right and therefore we must decide what to focus on—and what we're willing to give up to commit to a regular, meaningful practice. Then, and only then, will every session be an act of going back to the art of noticing what draws your attention and going deep into that place.

9. **Practices require payment.** All practices and habits have multiple outcomes over time. Practices that are easy to establish up front usually have a positive outcome in the short term, and a negative outcome in the long one. Take smoking cigarettes, for example—get a buzz and socialize with other folks in the courtyard at lunch up front. Lung cancer later. On the other hand, consider working out. There's actual pain involved at the beginning of engaging in that practice. Your muscles hurt on days one, two, and three. And yet, your body doesn't visibly change, the scale stays the same, and it's not for weeks or months later that you see any of the results you seek. More wisdom from habit guru James Clear: "The cost of your good habits is in the present. The cost of your bad habits is in the future." Be conscious of whether you're paying now or paying later.

10. **Discard the practices you don't want.** We adopt so many practices because of the default set of current circumstances in our lives—or hell, even in our culture. On one end of the spectrum, drinking alcohol to excess has been normalized. On the other, avoiding a "risky" career as an artist has been normalized because of the toxic (and false!) myth of

the starving artist. Building our practices on the beliefs of other people is dangerous, especially for those who have a history of playing it safe. You've just taken the word of others at face value for far too long. A dictum supposedly uttered by Socrates comes to mind: "The unexamined life is not worth living." Be aware. Be grateful for the present moment, but remember what got you here and, separately, what will get you to where you want to be.

Fire and Grace

Few people have lived the idea of practice as bravely and purely as the late Maya Angelou. In the dim light of nearly every dawn for decades on end, she sat alone in a cramped hotel room, as the soft hum of the city filtered in through the window. Her room was a sanctuary, a refuge from the cultural complexities of the outside world—and a place where Angelou could retreat into the depths of her imagination, to give voice to the stories that dwelled within her.

Despite the demands of her busy life, she made it a priority to carve out time for writing every day. With reassured hands, she made the habit of reaching for her worn typewriter, the keys smooth from years of use. It was her instrument, her conduit to the world—a faithful companion that bore witness to her joys and sorrows, triumphs and defeats. For Angelou, writing was not just a vocation but a sacred ritual—an act of self-discovery and catharsis. She famously rented the hotel room to fully immerse herself in her work, because she loved the process and ritual of writing. She described it as sacred to her as any religious ceremony—as something that sustained her, nourished her, and gave meaning to her existence.

But Angelou's creative writing practice was not just about the act of writing—it was about the art of living through her writing. As an icon of literature, she was just as committed to the daily process of writing at a particular time, in a particular place, as she was to the fundamentals of language and style, constantly honing her craft through study (she spoke six languages) and the development of her characters and narratives. It's been said that Angelou would often sketch out detailed outlines and character profiles before diving into the writing process, ensuring that she had a clear road map for the story ahead.

Everything was in order.

She has also confirmed, in interviews with Oprah Winfrey and others, that many of the elements in her work were direct reflections of her innermost thoughts and feelings, a mirror she held up to the complexities of the human condition. Her identity—both as a writer who had a responsibility to tell stories that needed telling *and* as a representative subject of her stories—often meant exposing her own vulnerabilities, and yet she moved through the world with grace.

Despite working so diligently in a small, dimly lit room for years on end, she was a light to so many of her readers and fans. Oprah shared, upon Angelou's death in 2014, "She was there for me always, guiding me through some of the most important years of my life. The world knows her as a poet but at the heart of her, she was a teacher . . . she will always be the rainbow in my clouds."

For Maya Angelou, there were no shortcuts to her writing

practice. In order to be the noun, she simply did the verb. What stands out so clearly now in hindsight, however, is that she knew full well the noun that she wanted to be—and that's exactly what she became.

Hard to Be What You Can't See

When W. Kamau Bell was a kid, he wanted to be a superhero— until he saw Eddie Murphy perform. That changed everything. "My mom said she could make me do anything if she promised to let me watch *Saturday Night Live*," he recalled to me, which was at the time the most readily available place to watch Eddie Murphy's comic mastery in action.

Fast-forward a couple of decades, and a friend told Kamau about an open-mic night down the street from his apartment in Chicago. It took him months to work up the nerve to try. But once he did, Kamau never looked back. Stand-up comedy was a passion, but it also terrified him, and at first success was just being able to get up on stage and take a swing at a thing he loved. Kamau discovered that it was a privilege to simply get to work.

In those early days, he went to his day job, then went on-stage late at night, where he had to deal with people mercilessly heckling him. For years. At the time, he was embarrassed to even call himself a comic, and he described failing over and over again. But he was determined to keep going. "You've got to jump in with two feet," he told me. "If you do it once every now and again, you're never going to find out if you're any good at it or if you love it. Whatever it is, you really have to dedicate some time to it. The thing about stand-up comedy especially is that stand-up doesn't actually want you to be a comedian. Stand-up comedy is like 'we're full' . . . so you have to really go for it."

Another stand-up comic—Nate Bargatze—once told me, "If you never see someone make it, then you think it's impossible. That's why people think it's impossible to [reach your dreams and] become famous, because they've never seen someone become famous." I spent some time with Nate in 2019, right after he'd just had a big Netflix special blow up. He told me he was still aware of how far he had to go, and he spent a fair bit of time talking about Kevin Hart doing arenas while he was still working in small theaters and comedy clubs, even though it was clear he was on the rise.

"Wherever I'm at," he said, "there's always a level above me."

What I remember noticing at the time—long before this book was even a twinkle in my eye—was that he seemed to be operating from the *identity* of a professional, stand-up comedian who loves his life and sells out arenas. I could smell it on him. It was not the least surprising to me, then, when just a few short years later, Nate began selling out the same arenas he once talked to me about—with his wife and daughter by his side, exactly how he'd described it.

But what if even this level of creative, professional, and personal transformation feels limiting to you? Maybe you can see yourself as a Michelin-star chef or a stand-up comedian who sells out arenas, but how might we go bigger in life or different or even more specific? Or what if we're still blocked, stifled, and playing it safe? How can we craft an even richer, more dynamic and dimensional identity for ourselves that doesn't already exist in the world? How do we even begin?

This, it turns out, is the most important creative process we will ever undertake—*if* you have the courage to pursue it. Yes, it's difficult to be what you cannot see, but this is precisely the point of the creativity within you. It all begins with your imagination.

Imagination + Action = Identity

What do you want to be when you grow up? From an early age, your parents and the generations ahead of you asked you that question—and I'm guessing that even my conjuring up of this memory floods you with the responses you uttered as a kid. Whatever they were, they were statistically most likely professions you were exposed to as a youngster. Just like that—and without any inkling of ill will—the conditioning began. We really have no one to blame for this. It started out as a game. The set of conditions—where you were born, to whom, your socioeconomic status, your gender, and any other number of similarly filtered factors—all played into your answer, whether knowingly or not.

But here is where all this nonsense must stop. If you fundamentally believe that the circumstances around your birth are the limiting factor on what's possible for you, then you will be correct. But I'd challenge you to think otherwise.

In filmmaking, we'd call this moment in the book "a pregnant pause." The camera zooms in on the protagonist (that's you), and we all, and especially you, the star of the show, know what must be done. It's suddenly clear that your entire life—

and by extension this entire book—has been in preparation for this moment, to make you aware and give you a not-so-gentle nudge in the direction of your dreams.

You see, all the examples I've used in this book are just that: examples. Of course, I encourage you to become a race car driver or a Michelin-star chef or an entrepreneur or a stand-up comic—*if* that is your dream. There are recipes for that in this book, and it's not an accident that I've sprinkled the stories of dozens of famous, iconic people throughout. Many of them started on their journeys just as you are now—some in a much more difficult spot. Perhaps you want to be like them—wherever they are now—standing on a stage, basking in the limelight, and living a similar dream.

Or not.

That is precisely why you've been blessed with an incredible imagination. There are ingredients in this book for dishes that have never been cooked. The stitches in the fabric of your life might be inspired by others, but the garment you're making is cut from your special cloth. And to be abundantly clear, none of this is about a particular profession, a specific title, fame, or fortune. All that focus is from the old model. This isn't about being a second-rate version of someone else. It's about being a first-rate version of you.

The *only* you.

This is about freedom. This is about choosing your life and how you live it. This is a journey of you shifting from always playing it safe, to taking an active role, designing, creating, deciding, and creating again; consistently practicing how you want to show up in the world. How you extend your life force out into the universe, whether that's a huge, loud life or a quiet, still one, is up to you. All, some, or none of it. A mixtape of your making.

Want a tiny experiment that will show you where to begin? Try this: Every day for thirty days straight, write down what you want and how you want to be. Simple. Commit to taking no longer than two minutes for this exercise. Just check your gut and spit out an answer. Every day, refine it. Get clearer and take action toward your answer.

In other words, this exercise is not concerned about your dreams being made up of this or that; big, small, or otherwise. What matters is simply that you start. What matters is that you no longer get talked out of living your dreams by all the other people who have given up on theirs.

As much as I can appreciate—and respect—what you've been through up to now in your life, this book you've picked up has the simple (albeit substantial) duty to remind you that your past is virtually irrelevant for who you actually "are" and where you're going; more importantly it has zero bearing on who you can become and what you can create. Your life— whatever remains of it, whether days or decades—will always be pure possibility. It doesn't matter how you got here. The fact is simply that here you are.

The danger now lies in avoiding the planning abyss—no more overthinking. Instead of ruminating on the perfect time, the perfect place, or the ideal ingredients for an error-free next step, simply begin to practice doing you. You have the tools within you to create the leverage you seek. Imagine the joy of reflecting on every imperfect step. It's the next one hundred tiny, creative strides that are the stepping-stones to your becoming.

Want to be exceedingly well understood by everyone around you? Be average. Want to be "realistic"? Go back to page one and review "Read This First" again. This is not an exercise in rationalism. You are now at the part where you must make a new shape for the contours of your life—from here on out.

Picking Up the Pieces

I had to take the meeting. What other choice did I really have?

In addition to being smart and experienced, Seth is an extraordinarily gracious person, who always has time for his friends and colleagues. Never pushy, always on point—and to the point. This is why, when he said, "Chase, I heard you sold the company. We should get together and talk," I accepted.

I know you've had moments like this—when you're agreeing ahead of time to what you know will be a tough conversation. It's like setting up a dentist appointment for a root canal, except instead of being aware of the forthcoming drill in your mouth, you're aware of the emotional land mines up ahead. You know it's necessary, inevitable even; nonetheless, the anticipation feels like waiting in line at the DMV. It was *that* kind of a premonition in my body.

I really couldn't say no, so right then and there we agreed on a time and place to get together the following day, Monday.

Later that day, I headed out for a "Walk & Talk." This is a weekly, Sunday afternoon heart-to-heart I've had with my wife, Kate, for more than a decade. During those check-ins, we share what's going on for each of us—the good, the bad, and

the ugly. I credit it with saving our marriage more than once—
it's a practice I highly recommend. Down the street to the city
park, around the small lake we go. It takes just under an hour.

We were not three minutes into this walk when Kate asked,
"Are you okay, honey? You've seemed a bit distant lately." I could
feel her looking gently in my direction, but I kept walking,
smiling softly, eyes straight ahead in line with my steps as we
continued on together. Her question struck me as not that out
of place, for after all, we're extremely open in our lives together,
our sharing and our caring—so it's not that uncommon for a
check-in question to be that direct. Also, I forgot to mention,
Kate is a coach and a mindfulness *teacher* (!!), so take that for
what it's worth. She's like a fucking laser beam for this stuff.
The kindest laser beam of all time, but a laser beam nonetheless.

I scratched my chin. And then spent the next thirty minutes
yammering rapid-fire about the past eighteen months, complete
with hand gestures, head nods, and voice inflections. One of
those conversations where you're like, "No. I mean, yes, every-
thing is good. Fine, I mean. Thank you," and then you talk
fire-hose style for a half hour straight without the other person
saying a word.

I recapped for her in a very logical, play-by-play sort of way
all of the major markers that had occurred in my life since
CreativeLive had been acquired.

*The public stock of our parent company went up on the
announcement of our acquisition—so, hey, that sure said
good things about us and the deal. And, while some of our
investors didn't do well, others did—and at least everyone
on the team has been well looked after. It was a special honor*

to notify employees who had worked for us for a long time that many of them would be receiving meaningful checks for all the hard work they'd put in. No private jets for our family, so that's a bummer, but all in all, we did okay and what an amazing ride it was. It was totally worth it. And yeah, I'm sad to say goodbye to my company, the investors, the millions of student customers, but it's not bittersweet— midway through the pandemic was the right time to sell an online learning platform, plus it was time to move on. Yeah, then there was the requisite year I'd promised to spend as an executive inside the "mother ship"—a sarcastic term we used for the buyer—transitioning our startup to operate inside the bigger, public company. Even though the promises made to us through the process of the transaction had not been kept, everything was fine, and it made it that much easier to leave the company after the year I had committed to. In fact, it was even slightly better than expected because I was able to score a three-month Garden Leave—which is a fancy term for staying on the payroll for administrative purposes while having no responsibilities. It sure was great that I'd been able to negotiate all that. And now it's been great to get to think about what's next . . .

"So yeah—I'm all good, honey, thanks for asking. How about you?" And by the way, I was quite certain that I had been very convincing in all this.

Then there was a very long pause. I mean, really long.

She looked straight ahead as we kept walking side by side. And what she said cut through me like Neil Diamond's "Sweet

Caroline" cuts through a karaoke bar.

"I'm worried about you, honey. It's been a while since I've seen you like this."

Fast-forward to the next day.

As you may have guessed by this point, Seth was on to me like white on rice. But not in a mean or condescending way. Quite the contrary. In the space of twenty minutes, he asked me a lot of questions about my life, and by the time I was done answering them, I could tell that *he* could tell I was a bit of a wreck. Not in the Rosanne Barr sort of way, but a more dangerous one where you look okay on the outside, but things are not well (ahem . . . a disaster) on the inside.

Fortunately for me, Seth is a superninja of sorts. He's lived a rich and meaningful life. He's built a number of giant communities on the internet, he's built and sold a few companies, has written eight thousand blog posts, nineteen bestselling books on creativity and entrepreneurship, and had a few public failures. He's in the Guerrilla Marketing Hall of Fame, the Direct Marketing Hall of Fame, and, just recently, the plain old no-modifier Marketing Hall of Fame. The guy knows how to communicate.

He diagnosed me within five seconds of my answering his last question.

"There's a hole in you that needs to be filled," he said. "And only you can fill it." He was right. And he was kind enough to share with me that he'd been there too, at an analogous time in his own life.

Between Kate and Seth, in the space of twenty-four hours, the lie that I was telling myself had been shown to me for exactly what it was. I was *not* fine.

At first, upon realizing this, I was heartbroken. I'd done it again. I had retreated from my life, betraying myself in the process as I'd done a few times before. Even worse, I had also vowed to never let it happen again. Yet there it was—or rather *here I was*—playing it safe. *Again!*

I had forgotten how to trust myself. Like a frog in boiling water, everything was fine until it wasn't. I had given up my power without even noticing.

After my chat with Seth, I sat in my car, staring through the windshield into the midmorning sunshine. I reviewed and I recapped how many times I'd run this cycle of abandoning myself before. Starting back in second grade—becoming self-aware and getting talked out of living bravely—doing magic tricks, comic strips, and stand-up routines, so I could be a cool kid. Feigning effortless brilliance in high school when I really gave everything I could to land a soccer scholarship. Again after undergrad, ignoring my creative calling and trading it in for $100,000 in student debt and debilitating illness. And again just a few months prior, selling my startup to the big public company either too late or too soon, it was hard to tell.

In any case, I'd done it again.

I'd allowed my attention to be hijacked.

There was never enough time.

I was ignoring my intuition.

Constraints had kept me down.

Play was always second to work.

I became scared to fail.

And I had forgotten the lessons I'd learned before about

practicing all of this.

And then by the grace of all that is magic in this world, I caught myself.

Hey, wait a minute. I have recovered from all of those missteps in my past.

Every single one of them.

Why am I counting all the times I fell down instead of all the times I got back up?

In Buddhism there's a concept called the second arrow, which encapsulates a profound truth about human suffering and the nature of our response to adversity. At its core, the first arrow represents the inevitable pain and challenges that life throws our way—the mistakes we make, the hardships we endure, the disappointments we face. We are shot with a metaphorical arrow in the back. And yet, these are the natural consequences of living in this beautiful, imperfect world, and while they may cause us pain, they are an unavoidable part of the human experience.

The second arrow, however, is an arrow of our own making, and most often is the arrow that causes the greatest harm when it hits us. This second arrow represents the self-inflicted suffering that arises when we judge ourselves harshly, criticize ourselves relentlessly, and dwell on our mistakes after they have already passed. It is the voice in our heads that tells us we are unworthy, unlovable, or inadequate because of our perceived failures. In other words, the second arrow is the completely unnecessary suffering we impose upon ourselves through our own negative self-talk and self-judgment.

It was at this moment, sitting in my car alone, that I caught myself before the second arrow hit, and I recognized the second arrow for what it was—a temporary product of my own mind. In paying attention to the first arrow, I managed to avoid the second.

It was then that I felt it. A spark of pride and gratitude.

Come to think of it, not only had I played through those letdowns and self-betrayals in the past, but they'd become less frequent in my adult life. The pain I'd felt in my soul—loss after selling the company and losing myself for a while—that pain I realized was just my soul trying to get my attention and trust it once again. Right there in my car in the sunshine on that Monday, I remembered that I had leverage over all this stuff that I'd been navigating. Everything I needed was already within me.

So I put the car in gear, checked my side mirror, pulled out into traffic, and headed for home, with a ray of hope and a commitment to get back to basics.

And, as if all that drama weren't enough, I couldn't help but smile later that same night when I found something scribbled in a journal that I'd remembered seeing online at some point before. Who knows where. No attribution. In my own terrible chicken-scratch handwriting it said:

Our initial identities in this world are first drafts that are written for us by other people from the time we were born. Hemingway said all first drafts are shit. So write another draft.
Get going. The time is now.

So that is exactly what I did.

Conclusion

A Life Played Well

If you recall from the introduction, Ghanaian photographer Paul Ninson had made it.

After nearly a decade of struggle, he had finished the program at the International Center for Photography; amassed a long list of top-tier commercial clients, including many of the world's leading brands in the pharmaceutical, energy, tech, and advertising sectors; and secured key roles in the hypercompetitive world of photo and video production in New York City. He was the successful professional creative he had always longed to become.

It wasn't just that Paul had left home and learned a craft. It was that he had taken a bold leap from a small village in Africa, made his way across the globe to one of the most difficult-to-navigate cities in the world, had become world-class at that craft, *and* had achieved professional success on many levels, especially when it came to providing financial support for his daughter back in Ghana.

In short, though the world had laughed at his dreams, he

had realized them *and then some*—against incredible odds. Paul was a shining example of what's possible when one refuses to play it safe.

During those ten years, Paul used all the levers we've talked about in this book. He stayed focused on his big-picture goal but also spent time and attention on learning every aspect of photography he could, including paying enough attention to spot Brandon in Accra. He followed his inner compass in an unconventional, some might have even said impractical, direction. He coped with considerable obstacles to success, but the constraints he faced forced him to get clear about what he wanted and ultimately got him to New York. He played, experimented, and "failed" again and again, going to the meeting of professional photographers and to Kenya with nothing to show for either trip . . . at first. But most of all, he had combined all the levers into a life of practice.

How much courage did it take? No more or less than you have right now. . . . *but* this isn't the end of Paul's story; it's the beginning.

You see, while Paul was attending to both the internal work of developing his skills and reawakening the tools within him and the eternal work of becoming the photographer and person he knew he could become, he was simultaneously working toward two new, even larger, dreams. First, he wanted to return home to his daughter, not only to provide for her financially but also to be fully present for her as a parent. Second, Paul wanted to transform photography in Africa. As you might suspect by now, both of these dreams have also come true.

"I want to build more than just a library. I want to build an entire learning center. A home for photography in Ghana," he decided. "There will also be a lecture hall where photographers from all over the world can come and teach. African photographers, especially. Who can teach African kids to tell African stories. There will never be another Paul Ninson. Who has to leave home, and feel this way, just to learn how to tell stories."

After graduation but before moving back to Ghana, Brandon and Paul launched a crowdfunding campaign. It just so happens that good things do often happen to good people.

The campaign raised more than $2.5 million, which immediately went to use in creating Paul's newest dream: Dikan Center, a celebrated institution that not only contains the largest photo library in Africa but also hosts exhibitions, education programs, public programs, and community-building initiatives centered around visual storytelling, leadership, and opportunities for anyone, especially young people, interested in changing the world.

Today, Paul is living the latest version of his dream, again something he accomplished by simply applying the tools we've discussed in this book. Dikan Center has become a renowned destination for artists, celebrities, tourists, and politicians traveling to Ghana, all of whom marvel at what Paul created from scratch. There is even a one-year photography program, modeled on the ICP program, a nod to the place where Paul learned so many essentials of the craft but also where he first decided that no African photographer should ever have to travel abroad again to live their dream of telling African stories with a camera.

Paul has not only built a life for himself and for his daughter, Ella; he's shown other young African photographers, educators, and artists—and the world—what's possible.

Though no one will follow exactly in his footsteps, Paul is a living example and has demonstrated without a doubt that we all have the tools we need inside us to get started today on a life we love—even in the face of incredible odds. Once a young man wrought with despair and saddled with the burdens—cultural, financial, shame, guilt, and more—that keep so many amazing humans from the life they deserve, Paul pushed through. In a world that's optimized for survival, Paul found creativity, happiness, joy, connection, harmony, fulfillment, and so many other of the gifts that he was eager to give as well as receive. He did it not just with luck or even skill. He did it with the tools available inside him.

He did it by refusing to play it safe.

It Begins with Belief

Archimedes had a powerful belief—an understanding—of what his unique experiences, capabilities, intuitions, and skills could accomplish. That is, when compiled, assimilated, and put into action. He knew that with the right tools and perspective, powered by his own imagination, he could do just about anything. And he was right.

The same is true for you.

Through living a life only *you* have lived—with all its nuances, twists, and turns—you have come to see the world from a unique point of view. Some things may be challenging for you, whereas others may come more easily. In some areas, you might be able to combine resources to overcome difficult problems in ways that others find mystifying. This is your personal creativity at work, applied in spaces where you have aptitude and a fair bit of practice accumulated.

In the same way that Archimedes combined a variety of tools, disciplines, and the brilliance of his own mind to not just accomplish incredible feats of engineering, but literally change the course of his life and the world, we can refuse to play it safe and leverage our creativity to solve all kinds of difficult problems. You, too, have parallel gifts that are worth combining in interesting ways and sharing with the world.

Like anything, this takes effort. No one knows everything, nor will anyone ever. And as you learn to use the tools covered in this book, you'll see that wins lead to more wins. Some may come more easily than others, but there is always something for you to learn. That's when even the failures feel less like an ass-kicking and more like a worthwhile lesson.

The most important thing to remember is that when we understand how to use what lies within and take action on that knowledge, we become more creative and powerful than we can imagine. We unlock the innate confidence and strength we need to do incredible things. Without belief, though—in ourselves and about what could be—it will be hard to get moving. Imagination and action build momentum and guide us in the direction of our dreams.

New Horizons

It's Monday morning. I have nowhere to be, nothing to do. I left the company I sold nearly a year ago. I've started working again, tinkering on some new business ventures and creating a TV show for a streaming service, but I'm taking the day off. I'm up at the beach house, and my schedule is open. My wife is on a meditation retreat, and the puppy we adopted a year ago is about to turn one. In fact, it's his birthday.

Kate and I never had children, so getting this pup was a big deal for both of us. Dogs and children aren't the same thing, of course; but this guy is a special part of our family. Throwing on a pair of swim trunks and slip-on Converse low tops I don't mind getting dirty, I call Bodhi, and he meets me at the back gate. We walk to the beach at a lazy pace.

This is the Pacific Northwest, so the "beach" is gray and rocky, and the ocean floor is covered with smooth, round stones that do more than massage your feet. Leaving my shoes on, I pull off my shirt, pick up a big piece of driftwood, and chuck it into the ocean. This is not our first rodeo. He knows the drill.

We sprint into the chilly water that never gets too warm, racing in the direction of the horizon to get the stick. He arrives first and grabs it with his teeth. Floating beside him, I pry the driftwood out of his mouth and toss it again across the surface of the water.

As we play this game, I think about my life and what's next. My wife, though not physically present, is here with us. We've been through so much together, the two of us—so many ups and downs, far too many lessons to count. We've seen failure, success, confusion, frustration, love, joy, peace, heartache, all of it. The strength of our relationship and her support has made it possible for me to return to myself again and again, to avoid playing it safe, knowing that whatever "home" I found when I followed my intuition, she would always be there. It occurs to me, as my body is suspended in the salty sea, that *this* right here is what it was all for. This contentment paired with an omnipresent sense of possibility. After all the work, all the struggle and celebration, I'll do my best to beat back my fear from now on and never play it safe again. I've arrived in the present moment with all its uncertainty and possibility. I can just be.

This is what it means to play by my own rules. I don't need to get somewhere else, move ahead, or achieve some grand accomplishment. It's about being free to be who and how I want to be. There is work to be done, even bills to pay, but today—right now—I float with my dog, drifting in the water, staring off at the horizon. I don't know what tomorrow will bring, and I'm happy to not know. For the first time in a very long time, I am content with the mystery and not planning my next move.

Of course, there will be more moves. We are all artists creating our lives and most of us are time billionaires, after all. There will be another moment right after this one. There will be more work, more highs and lows and opportunities to grow. But right now, I feel grateful and fulfilled.

A friend recently reminded me that Matthew Weiner, the creator of *Mad Men*, said after his hit show ended, "I just want my characters to be a little more happy than they were in the beginning. . . ."

I get that.

Life is a game where we are only ever playing against ourselves. For a long time, I reached for satisfaction through accomplishment. I wanted to beat the game, ace the test, win the race. And now—even if it's just for this one moment—it seems so simple. I can just be here, with the tools I have and internal resources I've developed. Instead of trying to get somewhere, to arrive at some other point, I have created where I am right now. And what I want is to be here.

I am far from enlightened and still full of all kinds of petty bullshit. Life is hard, or at least it can be. It's full of ups and downs and straight-up terrors. But I've learned that never playing it safe is an inside job. It's about figuring out who you are, what you most deeply desire, and using the resources available to move forward.

What we see projected before us is the culmination of what we've first imagined and then dared to create—the product of all the tools we've used to make something called a life. And today, as my dog swims up to give me a kiss on the face and I laugh out loud, it looks pretty good. I throw the stick again before we swim to shore for the short stroll home.

Acknowledgments

Every book is a journey, but this one felt different. Deeper. Further.

That's probably because after thirteen months of writing—and on the precipice of calling it *done*—I scrapped it all and started over. The previous book was shaping up fine. But *fine* was precisely the problem. It was acceptable. It was expected. It was a perfectly reasonable book about creativity and business—but it lacked soul and grit, risk, and a message that was capable of lasting impact; dare I say, transforming lives. And I couldn't figure out *what* it was lacking or *why* . . . until I got real honest with myself.

The truth that revealed itself during that inquiry was that the previous manuscript was playing it safe. *I was playing it safe.* Thus, it was this inward journey—into why I was choosing the predictable, well-worn, safe path instead of following my heart and the unknown—that ultimately gave birth to this book, the one I had been trying to write all along. When I shifted gears, I was terrified at first, but suddenly this book began spilling out of me like a cracked open bottle of champagne on New Year's Eve. It was yet another universal reminder that paying attention, trusting our intuition, failing, and starting anew—it all matters. All of the best stuff in life is on the other side of our fears.

So, in perhaps what might be a first in book acknowledgements, I want to start off by thanking myself for figuring this shit out—or rather *remembering*—just what we are capable of. *<Pats self on back. Shoutout to Snoop Dogg.>* Nice job, self. I'm proud of this book and what it took to get here. Living proof that we all have this knowing inside us, and that when we trust ourselves, the universe rewards us.'

Next, my wife Kate. Thank you, my love, for all your help, always being such a comfort and a sage—except for those moments where I want to keep it safe again and you politely nudge me to keep going. In case you need to hear it again, you are a very talented editor. Also, you might not know it, but I kept a picture of you on my desk during most of the writing process to remind me that you've always got my back, and that I was writing simultaneously as inspired by you and for you. The lifetime we've been together helping one another get unstuck and connected to our dreams is one of my greatest joys. And I've already seen the seeds you planted long ago begin to sprout. May this next chapter of your life—and ours together—be even more bold and beautiful than the many we've already shared.

To my small-but-mighty family: thank you for your unwavering support, your love, all the fun and laughs we've had together along the way and all that which awaits in our future. XO.

To my dearest friends: the badasses, the icons, the inspirations, stars, leaders, heroes, mensches, and masters. How in the hell am I so blessed to call all of you smart talented MF'ers my pals, my homies, my ride-or-dies?! Thanks for always having my back. For every one of you who shows up in these pages—thank you for being open to sharing your wisdom with me. For those who don't show up here, consider yourself lucky for now ;) You know who you are—and you know you've helped me immensely along my journey. Beware though, I've got lots more books left inside me, so you're not off the hook just yet. Please however never stop being the shiny, loving, funny, heartfelt, earnest, amazing, and inspirational humans you are.

Special holler to my writing-guru friends who have helped me become a better writer. Whether you helped with this book in particular by receiving early drafts that shaped the arc of this project, or you've been a guide in other one-on-one capacities: thank you. Seth Godin, Brené Brown, Tim Ferriss, Robert Greene, Ryan Holiday, Julia Serebrinsky, Charlie Hoehn, Scott Aumont, Ben and Taylor Winters and Jeff Goins . . . the time you've spent with me on the craft of writing has been such a gift.

To my agent, Steve. Thank you so much for your always calm and steady presence and your genuine enthusiasm for this work. Having you in my corner makes it possible for me to do what I love and, in turn I hope, helps others do the same. And a special hat tip for helping me navigate the turbulence of chucking out the early version of this manuscript too close to deadline and believing in me to generate something new and fresh. That took guts, and I'm grateful. Here's to a long, bright future together.

To the entire team that worked on this book day in, day out, thank you. To Hollis, Milan, and everyone at Harper: thank you for believing in me and my crazy ideas. For going to bat for me in all the big meetings. All of it. Every one of our interactions shows me how much you care. BTW, given we're really getting a handle on this whole working together thing, I'm guessing we should do some more books together. To Julie Corotis—you're a legend. How did I get so lucky to get to work with you all these years? May it never end. Thank you. Nasa Koski, thank you for bringing all of your many talents to bear, including the hard work and the passion. Never forget how contagious it is. Julie Mosow: thank you so much for tapping in later in the game than was comfortable to make this dream come to life. Wow. You are awesome. I'm off-the-charts grateful for all your skills, caring, and kindness. This feels like the first of many projects together. Hat tip to David Moldawer for the intro. Vasco Morelli: Once again you brought the visual package together my friend. Thank you. I love where we landed and the process to get here was a treat. And to everyone else in the trenches making this happen . . . as I wrote in my previous book *Creative Calling*, community is king. It truly takes a village to pull together any creative project and this one yet again proves it out in spades.

Lastly—and on the topic of community—I am eternally grateful for every one of you in my worldwide creative community. Whether you've been aboard my bus for a day or a lifetime, I'm so very thankful to be on this journey together. I do a lot of this work for myself, but I'd be lying if I didn't say that I do a lot of it for—and with—you too. So many of you helped guide the writing, the titling, and the jacket cover design of this book with your feedback. I'll keep showing up for you, and I've got my fingers crossed that you'll keep showing up for me. Together, let's continue growing our posse and spreading the good word about what's truly possible on the points of freedom, creativity, and a life you love. Endlessly upward. Benevolent mischief. And remember: in order to become the noun, just do the verb.

Much love,

Seattle, WA
Sunday, April 21, 2024

About the Author

CHASE JARVIS is an award-winning artist, entrepreneur, and bestselling author. As one of the most influential photographers of the past twenty years, he has created campaigns for companies like Apple, Nike, and Red Bull. Galleries have exhibited his fine art in the United States, Europe, and the Middle East. He was a contributor to the Pulitzer Prize–winning *New York Times* story "Snow Fall" and earned an Emmy nomination for his documentary *Portrait of a City*. He created Best Camera, the App of the Year and the first photo app to share images to social networks. Chase was the founder and CEO of CreativeLive, where more than fifty million students learn photography, video, design, music and business from the world's top creators and entrepreneurs (acquired by FVRR: NYSE in 2021). He hosts the *Chase Jarvis LIVE* podcast, with more than fifty million downloads, and his last book, *Creative Calling*, debuted as a national bestseller.

Chase has been a keynote speaker on six continents, an advisor to *Fortune* 100 brands, and a guest at the Obama White House, the United Nations, the Library of Congress, 10 Downing Street, Buckingham Palace, and the DIFC in Dubai. Chase lives with his wife, Kate, and their dog, Bodhi, in Seattle, Washington, where he serves as a volunteer board director for several nonprofits. He is @chasejarvis on all social media platforms.

www.chasejarvis.com
www.neverplayitsafe.com